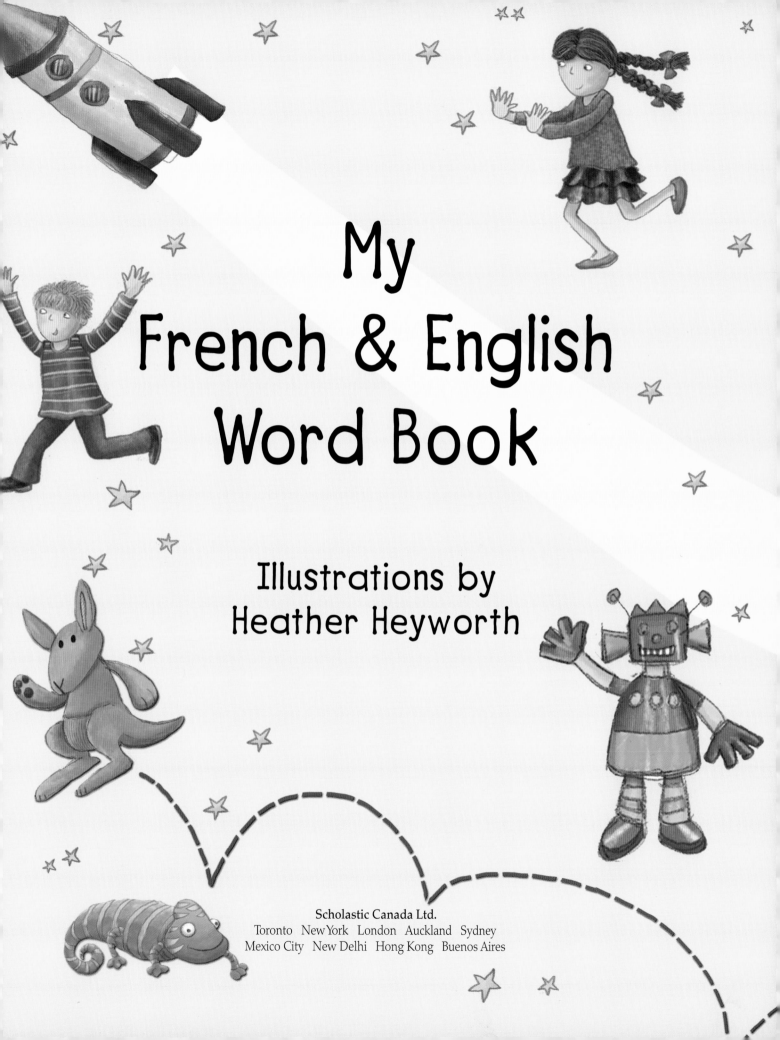

My
French & English
Word Book

Illustrations by
Heather Heyworth

Scholastic Canada Ltd.
Toronto New York London Auckland Sydney
Mexico City New Delhi Hong Kong Buenos Aires

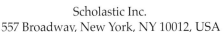

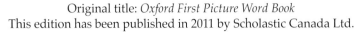

Scholastic Canada Ltd.
604 King Street West, Toronto, Ontario M5V 1E1, Canada

Scholastic Inc.
557 Broadway, New York, NY 10012, USA

Scholastic Australia Pty Limited
PO Box 579, Gosford, NSW 2250, Australia

Scholastic New Zealand Limited
Private Bag 94407, Botany, Manukau 2163, New Zealand

Scholastic Children's Books
Euston House, 24 Eversholt Street, London NW1 1DB, UK

Original title: *Oxford First Picture Word Book*
This edition has been published in 2011 by Scholastic Canada Ltd.

ISBN 978-1-4431-0931-4

Library and Archives Canada Cataloguing in Publication	Catalogage avant publication de Bibliothèque et Archives Canada
Heyworth, Heather My French and English word book / written and illustrated by Heather Heyworth ; French text by Isabelle Montagnier.	Heyworth, Heather My French and English word book / written and illustrated by Heather Heyworth ; French text by Isabelle Montagnier.
Text in English and French.	Texte en français et en anglais.
ISBN 978-1-4431-0931-4	ISBN 978-1-4431-0931-4
1. Vocabulary--Juvenile literature. 2. French language--Vocabulary--Juvenile literature. 3. Word recognition--Juvenile literature. I. Montagnier, Isabelle II. Title.	1. Vocabulaire--Ouvrages pour la jeunesse. 2. Anglais (Langue)-- Vocabulaire--Ouvrages pour la jeunesse. 3. Reconnaissance des mots--Ouvrages pour la jeunesse. I. Montagnier, Isabelle II. Titre.
PE1449.H49 2011 j428.1 C2011-900315-5E	PE1449.H49 2011 j428.1 C2011-900315-5F

The *Oxford First Picture Word Book* was originally published in English in 2011.
This edition is published by arrangement with Oxford University Press.

Scholastic Canada Ltd. would like to thank Lesley Pettitt for her help with text compilation.

Text copyright © Oxford University Press 2011
Illustrations © Heather Heyworth 2011
French text copyright © Éditions Scholastic 2011

5 4 3 2 1   Printed in China CP147   11 12 13 14 15

Welcome to this word book. Turn the pages to find words in familiar settings. You can spot all the words illustrated in the pictures, search for the chameleon hiding in every scene, and answer the robot's questions. You can enjoy this book in many ways—create stories, look at the details, and begin to recognize words for everyday favourite things, in French and in English.

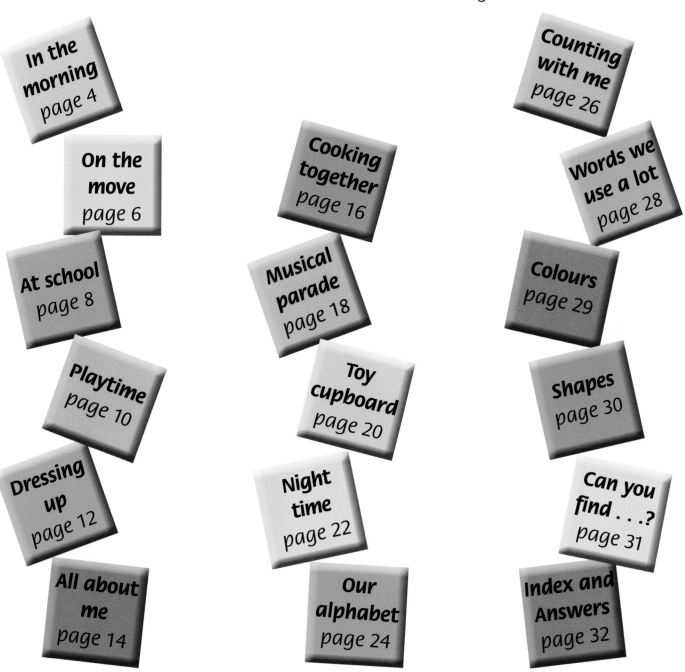

Le matin
In the morning

une camisole
undershirt

un tee-shirt
T-shirt

une chemise
shirt

un chandail
sweater

un short
shorts

un pantalon
pants

une jupe
skirt

une robe
dress

un chapeau
hat

un manteau
coat

une écharpe
scarf

un parapluie
umbrella

des gants
gloves

des chaussures
shoes

5

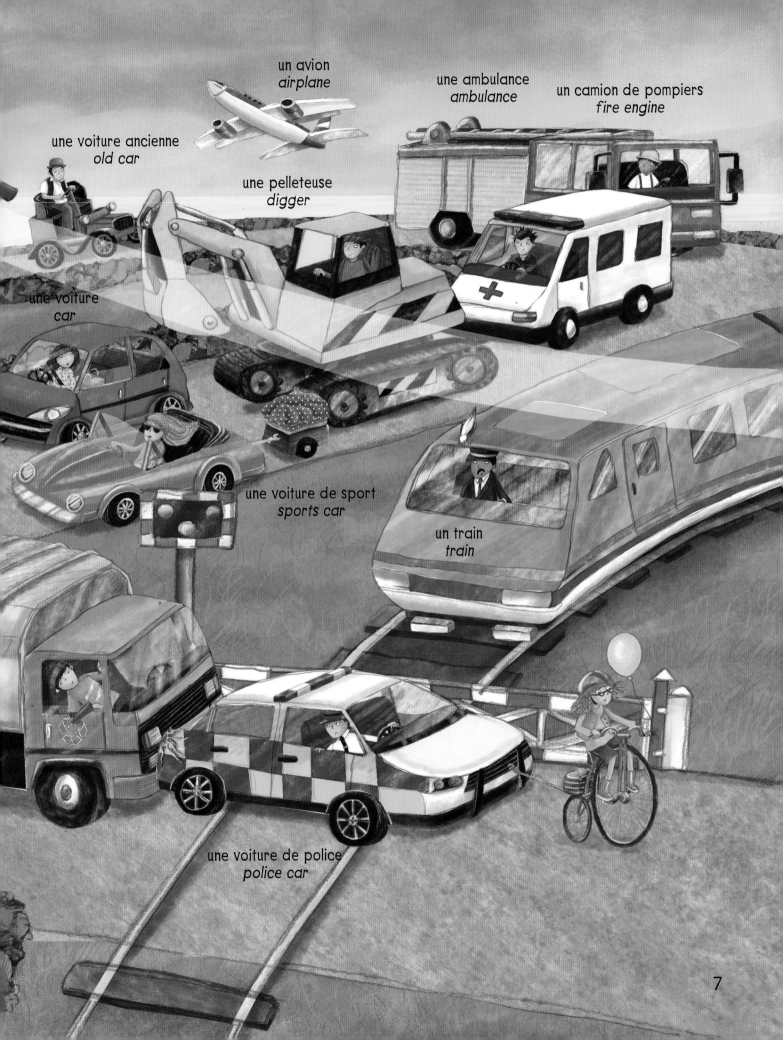

un avion
airplane

une ambulance
ambulance

un camion de pompiers
fire engine

une voiture ancienne
old car

une pelleteuse
digger

une voiture
car

une voiture de sport
sports car

un train
train

une voiture de police
police car

À l'école
At school

une boîte-repas
lunch box

des livres
books

sauter
à la corde
skip

courir
run

une enseignante
teacher

des crayons
de cire
crayons

What are the children painting?

8

sauter
jump

donner un
coup de
pied
kick

un ballon
ball

sautiller
hop

une table
table

une chaise
chair

de la colle
glue

des ciseaux
scissors

une règle
ruler

des crayons
pencils

un pinceau
paintbrush

de la peinture
paint

9

L'heure du jeu
Playtime

des graines
seeds

une pelle
shovel

une bêche
pitchfork

de la terre
soil

un arrosoir
watering can

une fleur
flower

une feuille
leaf

un chat
cat

un chien
dog

un papillon
butterfly

une coccinelle
ladybug

un bourdon
bumblebee

une fourmi
ant

un escargot
snail

une grenouille
frog

What makes a sunflower grow?

On se déguise!
Dressing up

Can you match all the different words to the costumes?

un joueur de soccer
soccer player

une princesse
princess

un pompier
firefighter

un fantôme
ghost

un médecin
doctor

une ballerine
ballet dancer

un astronaute
astronaut

un prince
prince

une policière *police officer*	un cuisinier *cook*	un chevalier *knight*	une cowgirl *cowgirl*	un constructeur *builder*
une vétérinaire *vet*	un pirate *pirate*	une fée *fairy*	un clown *clown*	un pilote de course *race car driver*

Me voici
All about me

le visage
face

la joue
cheek

l'oreille
ear

la langue
tongue

le nez
nose

le menton
chin

l'œil
eye

Pick a word and see if you can point at it in the picture!

le cou
neck

le bras
arm

l'épaule
shoulder

le coude
elbow

la main
hand

le doigt
finger

la poitrine
chest

le ventre
tummy

la jambe
leg

le genou
knee

le pied
foot

l'orteil
toe

15

Cuisinons ensemble
Cooking together

du beurre
butter

un couteau
knife

des œufs
eggs

du fromage
cheese

un bol
bowl

du pain
bread

une cuiller en bois
wooden spoon

de la farine
flour

de la pâte
pastry

16

Le défilé des instruments
Musical parade

une harpe
harp

une flûte
tin whistle

une trompette
trumpet

un triangle
triangle

une flûte à bec
recorder

des maracas
maraca

un banjo
banjo

What instrument is the boy in the red shorts playing?

un cor
horn

un accordéon
accordion

des cymbales
cymbals

un tambour
drum

des clochettes
bells

des castagnettes
castanets

une grosse caisse
bass drum

un chef d'orchestre
bandleader

19

Le placard à jouets
Toy cupboard

Which animals live in the sea?

un éléphant
elephant

un crocodile
crocodile

une girafe
giraffe

un poisson
fish

un perroquet
parrot

un kangourou
kangaroo

un singe
monkey

un koala
koala

une souris
mouse

un pingouin
penguin

un tigre
tiger

un zèbre
zebra

un panda
panda

un rhinocéros
rhinoceros

un serpent
snake

un cheval
horse

un hérisson
hedgehog

une pieuvre
octopus

un poulet
chicken

une araignée
spider

un ours
bear

21

Bonne nuit!
Night time

la lune
moon

une étoile
star

un vaisseau spatial
spaceship

une planète
planet

des rideaux
curtains

une garde-robe
wardrobe

un réveil
clock

un télescope
telescope

une serviette
towel

une baignoire
bath

un pyjama
pyjamas

une brosse à dents
toothbrush

un lit
bed

What can you look through to make the stars appear bigger?

23

L'alphabet
Our alphabet

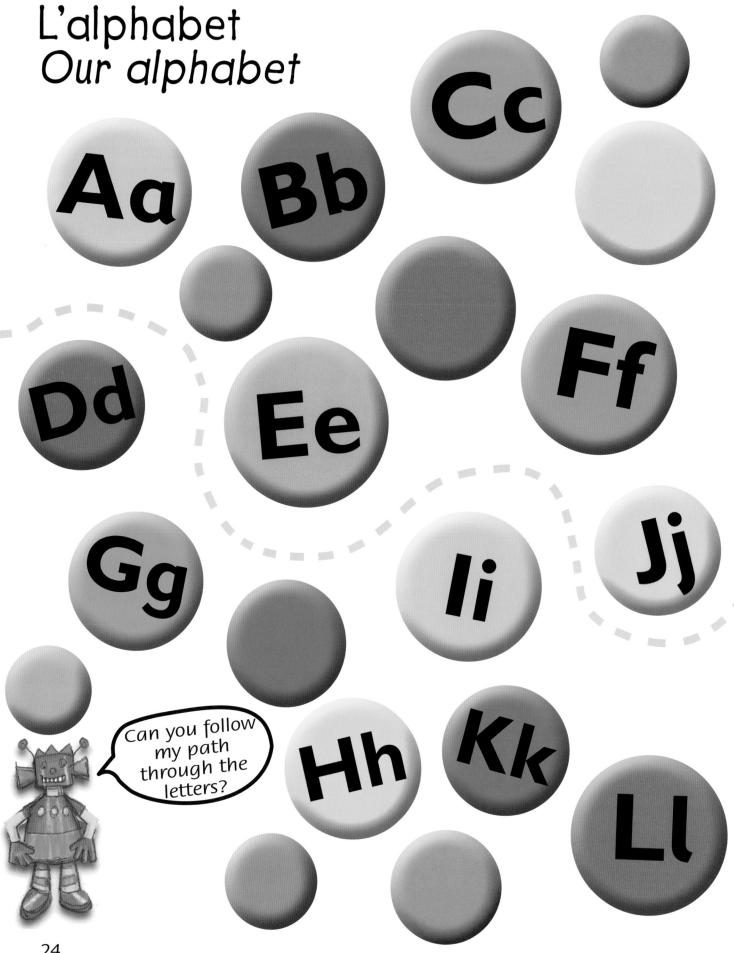

Can you follow my path through the letters?

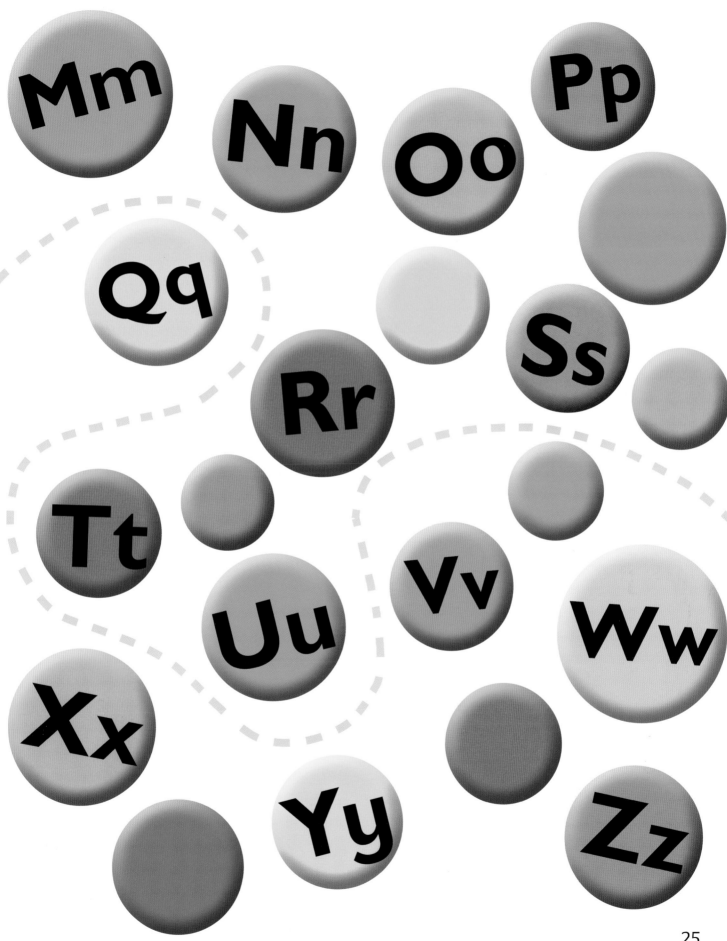

Compte avec moi!
Counting with me

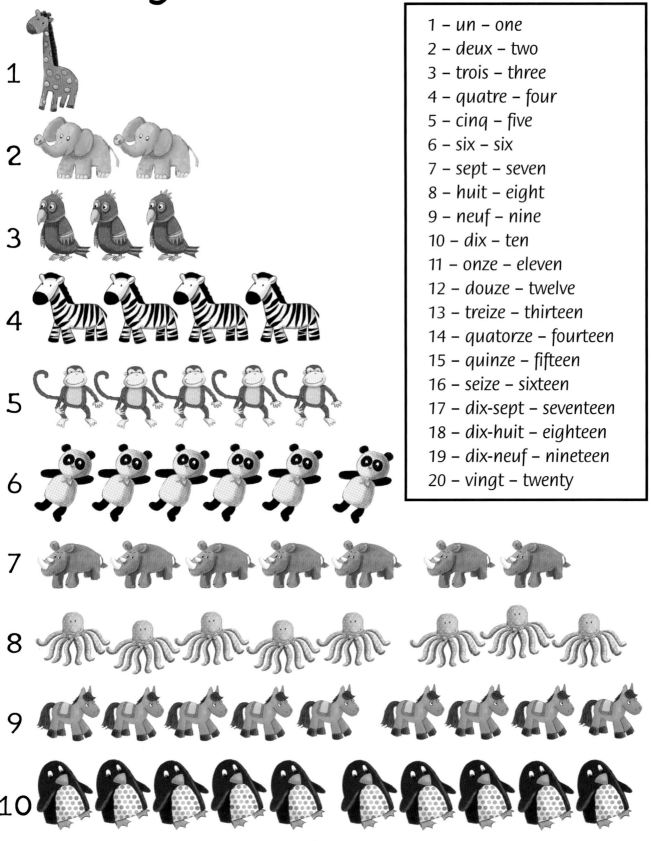

1

2

3

4

5

6

7

8

9

10

1 – un – one
2 – deux – two
3 – trois – three
4 – quatre – four
5 – cinq – five
6 – six – six
7 – sept – seven
8 – huit – eight
9 – neuf – nine
10 – dix – ten
11 – onze – eleven
12 – douze – twelve
13 – treize – thirteen
14 – quatorze – fourteen
15 – quinze – fifteen
16 – seize – sixteen
17 – dix-sept – seventeen
18 – dix-huit – eighteen
19 – dix-neuf – nineteen
20 – vingt – twenty

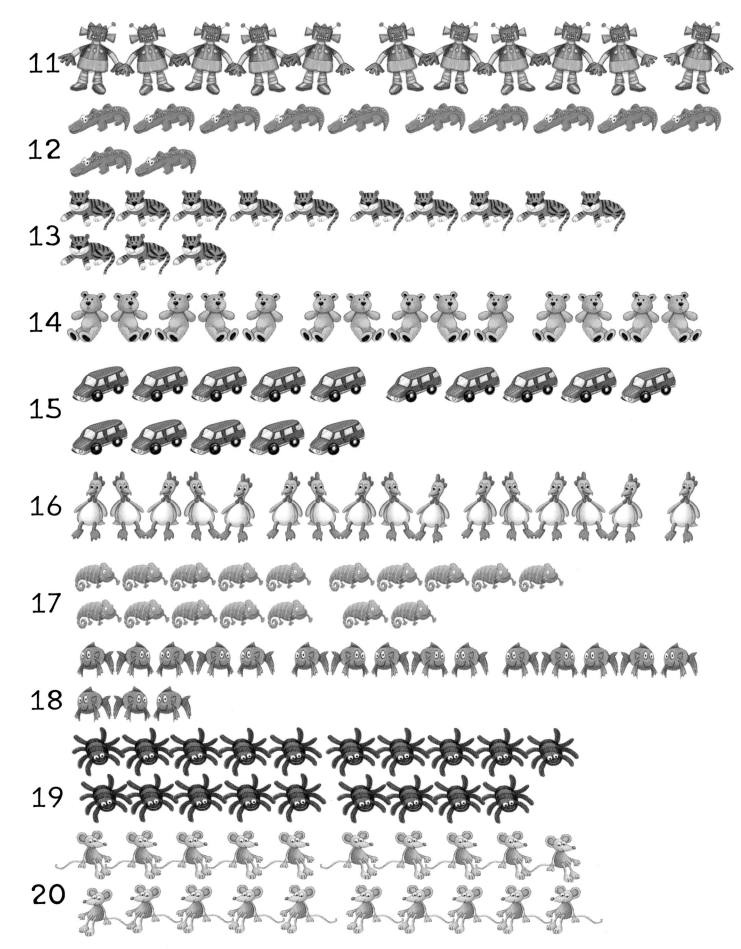

11

12

13

14

15

16

17

18

19

20

Les mots courants
Words we use a lot

a *has*	**je** *I*	**est** *is*	**elle** *she*	**dans** *in*	**non** *no*
oui *yes*	**vers** *toward*	**vais** *go*	**de** *of*	**nous** *we*	**me** *me*
suis *am*	**tu** *you*	**mon** *my*	**on** *we*	**elles** *they*	**il** *he*
chez *to*	**pour** *for*	**le** *the*	**et** *and*	**ils** *they*	**sont** *are*
la *the*	**va** *going*	**tout** *all*	**aime** *love*	**vois** *see*	**sur** *on*
	peux *can*	**jour** *day*	**joue** *play*	**ce** *this*	**as** *have*

How many words start with the letter "a"?

Table of Contents

Thanks

Great leadership is fun to watch and throughout my career I was able to learn firsthand from some of the best. Dianna Lindsay taught me how to set high expectations and shape school culture around doing what is right for children. She got me excited about leadership and helped me set a path. Getting people to work together can be challenging, and I could have not asked for any better coach and mentor than Rick DuFour. He guided me through the principalship using the lens of collaborative learning and sharing as the foundation for improving a school. Bill Sanders taught me how teacher variability is the most critical issue in schools and the number one problem for principals to resolve. And as I devote the remainder of my career to helping school leaders, crossing paths with Jack Grayson has been a blessing. A giant in the field of productivity and knowledge transfer, Jack has inspired me to help leaders utilize tools that capture the critical elements of best practices, so that schools can quickly ratchet up their improvement of teaching and learning in every classroom.

And, of course, pulling all of the content of this book together required a lot of support and tolerance from my family. Beth, Eric, Christina, and Chad are members of a generation that are determined to get it right. They serve as my source of energy to keep going at it each day. Betsy has been my unwavering partner and shares my passion to help schools get better. I love you all.

Finally, special thanks to Bob Sickles who has guided me through this project and serves as a model for publishers who look for new ideas and ways to share them for the common good.

Introduction

More than once in my career, I was handed a set of keys and a two-way radio at the beginning of a principalship. Were these the primary tools of school leadership? The first time it happened I took them in hand, as though a torch had been passed. I didn't know who to call on the radio. Telephones are standard equipment, but radios carry a sense of urgency. And what if someone called me asking for help? None of my graduate professors told me that I would be making decisions that fast. Why did I need all of those keys? I didn't want to look like I didn't know what to do, but you have to trust someone and so I sheepishly turned to my secretary for clarification. "Did the principal really fill the vending machines?" I asked. "Yes, he didn't trust this to anyone else and we rely on the profits of those machines to do things for the teachers and the school," she said. It took me 20 minutes to figure out how to open the machine, and an equal amount of time to determine the right slot for the Little Debbie snacks. It didn't stop with managing the machines. I learned that the principalship also included monitoring the cafeteria, checking restrooms, listening to personal problems of the faculty, and smelling the aroma of diesel as students raced to get on their buses. After everyone was gone I would walk the halls of my school and have a therapy session with one of my second-shift custodians in order to put myself back together before heading home or onto an evening school event. Each day was a whirlwind of issues, problems, and tasks that caused me to question what I was doing and how I would ever have an impact if I was constantly performing so many things that had little to do with teaching and schooling. I also discovered that my superiors were victims of the same set of expectations and that, over time, they too resembled managers, sitting on a mountain of duties, tasks, and responsibilities—managers overseeing other managers.

Such is the plight of so many principals and school leaders. In spite of numerous attempts to improve education, communities continue to believe that principals should perform a multitude of managerial tasks, and also find time to work with teachers to improve learning for all children. All of this comes at a time when schools need to prepare students for one of the most competitive eras of global economics. This book is about redirecting your leadership from traditional expectations to effective practices that will improve teaching and learning in your school. Whether you are a practicing administrator, new to leadership or preparing to lead, the processes presented in this book are applicable to you and grounded in numerous studies of school leadership, my own longitudinal research of school principals and principal interns, and years of personal experience in attempting to improve my own school leadership. The good news is that it is not too late to change the way you perform your daily work. Using processes that incrementally shift daily work habits into strategic areas of instructional leadership, you can make significant gains in your effectiveness, and more importantly, the academic success of your students.

I would be remiss if I did not provide one caution to your reading. This book is not a quick fix to the principalship. You won't lose old habits in a couple of weeks. It will be painful at the beginning and will require a considerable amount of self-discipline. But like a successful weight loss program, you will learn to shed administrivia through a focus on a healthy diet of instructional leadership and a lot of exercises to get you in shape and on the right path to better results, one day at a time.

Finally, school leadership is about passion for doing what is right for children, a clear vision of how to accomplish this, and most important, courage to act. This book will help you learn how to fight back and recapture precious time to lead. Instead of passively accepting more administrative tasks, you will behave like I did when my secretary filled the top of my desk with little envelopes of keys. "What's this?" I asked. "These are the keys that the principal distributes as the teachers arrive for the school year," she said. "Take them away and ask the custodian to come and see me," I said. You can do it too. Put down your radio and keys, and let's get started with your transformation.

Chapter 1

Why Change the Way I Lead?

There's only one corner of the universe you can be certain of improving, and that's your own self.

—ALDOUS HUXLEY

The answer to this question is essential because it provides the passion to first change yourself and in turn change others. Why change? First, our present system of education does not provide the quality of education that all children will need to advance in their studies, compete in a global economy, and enjoy a quality of life that is fundamental to our democracy. Second, national studies indicate that school principals spend a great deal of their time on duties and tasks that don't connect with the necessary leadership skills that bring about changes to education—most notably, improved teaching and learning (Archer, 2004; NASSP & Milken Family Foundation, 2001). Third, research tells us that school leadership can make a substantial difference in improving the education of students if it is focused on daily work that is directly involved in helping teachers improve what goes on in the classroom (Leithwood, Louis, Anderson & Wahlstrom, 2004; National Study of School Evaluation, 2005; Waters, Marzano & McNulty, 2003).

We are at an important crossroads in public education, and for the first time in our nation's history, what we are able to provide for our students will have a direct impact on their ability to sustain the American way of life. What is surprising is that many of our colleagues do not fully comprehend the speed and complexity to which the world is changing, and how our children will enter adulthood at a significant disadvantage if we fail to retool American education. School leadership finds itself at the center of this challenge.

Ask teachers why their school is engaged in changes and new initiatives and you will quickly understand their confusion. In many cases their responses will be both disappointing as well as revealing. Teachers feel disconnected from the improvements that school leaders have attempted to promote because we have not invested enough time in helping them understand the purpose behind

1

our motives. The mounting pressure from states and the federal government to improve academic results is not without foundation. For decades our country's leadership has called upon educators to improve education as the price and quality of labor has rapidly changed around the world. Yet, in many cases, educators continue to use as their frame of reference an outdated infrastructure that was designed to sort and select students for a postwar economy that no longer exists. In the fifties, the average dropout rate in the U.S. was around 50 percent. But for the most part, it didn't really matter as young adults with a strong back and work ethic could enter the marketplace and earn a decent wage to support themselves and a family. Those who were more advantaged, gifted, or motivated to continue their education pursued college degrees, many in the fields of science and mathematics. Issues such as poverty and inequality were raised, but for many Americans, life was good and parents were satisfied with the education being provided. Growing issues slipped under our radar and educators continued to operate with a false sense of affirmation that everything was working and that all students had some type of future beyond school.

As the conditions of the marketplace changed, pressure to improve our schools increased. But in many cases, we found ourselves ill equipped to provide a larger percentage of the population with a quality education that would enable students to succeed beyond high school. School administrators who were trained to manage buildings, budgets, and student discipline found themselves at a loss when it came to improving teaching and learning. In many cases, principals were hired based on a perception of their ability to control students and oversee school operations. Teaching was left up to teachers. Managing schools was more about efficiency and less about effectiveness.

When the school accountability movement took root in America, many school districts looked to successful business practices to guide them towards improvement. But when educators borrowed these practices, they took good ideas and misapplied them to school settings. Such was the case with strategic planning. School boards and superintendents gathered representative groups of staff, administration, parents, and community members and formed committees to determine the mission, vision, and issues they believed to be at the center of school improvement. The problem with this approach was that it became vision via consensus. The products of their work were often translated into plans that became less strategic and more closely aligned to the perceived issues of the day. Had we paid closer attention to strategic action as reported in works such as *In Search of Excellence* (Peters & Waterman, 1982), we would have learned that successful organizations wrap their plans around the customer, in our case, the students.

In a landmark article on strategic planning in schools, Mike Schmoker (2004) revealed how far removed the process drifted from the important work that principals and teachers must perform to improve learning for all children. He called upon schools to focus their attention on sustained cycles of improvement connected to collaborative work in curriculum, instruction, and assessment. In contrast, schools created strategic committees and action plans that redirected the energy of the school district to a wide variety of issues tangential to the core business and purpose of education.

This left principals and teachers on their own to improve the academic results of children. What typically followed was a series of well-intended initiatives that became short in life and void of improvement. Many principals who were already overwhelmed with responsibilities searched for quick fixes and delegated the establishment and implementation of new programs to teachers. Others spent considerable time and resources sending staff to workshops in hopes that people would learn something new to bring about better results. When student achievement results fell short of district expectations, central office administrators reacted by mandating improvements for all schools using one-size-fits-all programming. These types of efforts lacked a shared sense of purpose that was deeply rooted in an urgent need for change. It should be no surprise that teachers reacted by resisting change and clinging to the present. To them, change was something to avoid. To fix this, we first must take people back to why we need to change. This responsibility rests firmly on the shoulders of school leadership. Too often we assume that people see and understand the obvious, but organizational change underscores the need to repeatedly connect people with purpose.

Why American Education Must Change: What Leaders Need to Know

Leaders must have a passion for change before engaging others in a vision of what they want to accomplish. The source of this passion is a clear understanding of the conditions that present threats or opportunities for the school, and most importantly, the students. Becoming an expert on these issues is a prerequisite to leading with purpose. Without a solid understanding of the world our students will face, adults will simply continue to convince themselves that everything is fine. It is up to leadership to study these conditions and bring others to a common understanding of the purpose of their work.

I was blessed to have worked in some very good schools throughout my career in public education. Good teachers, supportive parents, and hard-working students provided a winning combination on these campuses. When I started in the profession, a certain number of my students had clear paths to college defined by parental expectations and a curriculum designed for that purpose. Others could not wait to finish their diploma and start their lives working and earning a wage. Some were quite glib in telling me that their grades were not that important because they could get an entry-level job at the local factory that would pay them more than my teacher salary. They were right. Times were good, and the prosperity of our country enabled an educational system to become satisfied with the status quo.

Now we find ourselves competing with China, India, Korea, Russia, and Eastern European countries where people are racing to capture what we as Americans have enjoyed for so many years. Where are they focusing their attention? They are retooling their education systems in tandem with the economic opportunities that present themselves in a new age world. In his book, *The World is Flat*, Tom Friedman (2007) devoted a chapter titled, *The Quiet Crisis*, in which he made a compelling case that the convergence of three issues within our present educational system will gather into a significant storm unless we make dramatic changes. First, he stated that we are not producing the rate of scientists, engineers, and mathematicians that were the foundation of the post-World War II economy in the U.S. Second, he provided evidence of an ambition gap and limited work ethic among American youth. Lastly, he pointed to a widening gap between the academic performance of our students and those in other countries.

How the Rules for Education Have Changed

Another way of explaining all of this is that after World War II our country enjoyed a tremendous era of sustained economic growth as soldiers returned home and went to work. American products ruled the marketplace and allowed companies to pay higher than average wages because the rest of the world wanted our products. But as the Cold War ended, countries that were underdeveloped for so many years realized that capitalism would allow their people to enjoy a better standard of living if they entered the race for economic supremacy. As they delivered cheap labor to the marketplace, the cost of producing products began to fall. American companies took advantage of this labor in order to compete and survive. Today, the old adage that a strong back and a good work ethic will bring you a wage that will support a family is no longer true. This is a rude awakening for an educational system that relied on the ability to sort and separate children into college-bound and labor-bound tracks. The real test of our present educational system is the degree to which we can provide students with an equal opportunity to acquire a quality education that will enable them to continue their education beyond high school, and successfully compete in a fast-changing global marketplace. Many in our profession have failed to come to grips with this reality, or simply want to dismiss it. The problem is that the race is on and we don't have time to debate, deny, or grieve over the good old days when less was expected. The march is on, and as school leaders we must be able to convey this information to staff over and over in order to connect them to the urgent need to find better ways to reach all kids.

Much of this sounds like a history lesson, but keep in mind that a typical faculty consists of a mix of veterans and those newer to the profession. Providing a historical context, along with a clear understanding of present and future conditions, will enable people to bridge the gap between where we came from and the challenges that confront our profession. The key issue for leadership is to not think that a single speech at a faculty meeting, a video, or a book study, will be sufficient to keep people connected to the urgency for improvement. School leaders must drive the need for change deep into the culture of the school in ways that keep a sense of urgency front and center.

Getting acquainted with the conditions and issues that build a passion for change does not have to be a daunting task. Start with the large, big-picture issues that our children will have to confront as adults. These alone make a solid case for improving education for all children. Although the list will vary depending on the sources you read, most authors agree on areas of concern including the globalization of the economy, the declining value of a high school diploma, the dropout rate, the poverty rate, and the equal playing field that technology has created for people in other countries who want to advance their education and training.

Local Issues to Examine

More than once I was faced with a faculty that had established a solid track record of success. How do you get people passionate about change when they feel satisfied with the results? Give them strong doses of reality. Most schools celebrate their success based on state assessment results, but if you take a closer look at the data, the results reveal significant gaps to be closed. First, most state assessments are designed to measure the minimum expectations of the state's curriculum and in fact measure these at basic levels rather than proficiency. Compare your state results against your state's averages on the National Assessment of Educational Progress (NAEP) and you will be surprised to see that a substantial gap exists. Second, a number of districts tend to play down the percentage of the student population that did not meet minimum state standards. We tend to celebrate an 80 percent passing rate while not showing concern for the one out of five children who were unable to make it over the bar.

Becoming an Expert on the Need for Change

As you begin to build your knowledge of the world that our children will face you will feel a passion for change begin to grow along with an expertise on these topics. Articles and reports in the news will grab your attention. Consider a report that was covered by *The Cleveland Plain Dealer* (10-24-07) announcing the opening of a new Wal-Mart. Four thousand residents filed applications for the 300 jobs to be filled. The average wage for these positions was less than 22,000 dollars a year—the poverty level for a family of four in the U.S. Stories like these have been around for a while but as you pay closer attention and look for evidence to share with your faculty you will find an unending supply of stories, reports, studies, and evidence that we are in a crisis that connects our ability to compete with our ability to educate. Now is the time to get passionate.

Taking Teachers Back to Why They Joined the Profession

I believe that the majority of teachers joined the profession because they possessed a strong desire to help children learn and succeed. Think of the compassion that teachers display when a student arrives at a classroom door on a set of crutches. Their reaction is immediate, sincere, and purposeful. They also feel a sense of urgency to improve conditions for the student. The challenge for school leadership is to replicate these feelings and behaviors by engaging teachers in a deep understanding of how disabled their students will become without an adequate education. Start with a faculty meeting and begin a dialogue on the numerous issues that should cause teachers to reconnect with their belief system. I have found it useful to have teachers present this information to their colleagues. But remember, once is not enough. As Friedman warned us, the storm is gathering, and therefore we need to keep educators focused on each weather report so that, over time, a passion for change and strong sense of purpose guides the daily work of the school. For several years I have shared need for change presentations with teachers, school leaders, and board members, and their reaction is always the same, "What can we do and how can we get started?" The answer is to start with a look at yourself before you lead others.

The Plight of School Principals

"Never become a school principal." Believe it or not, those were my father's words to me when I was a teenager. He served as a postmaster, and as is the case in small towns across America, the post office is one of those places where everybody gets to know everyone's business. He heard too many complaints about school principals and came to a conclusion that it was a thankless job, with long hours and little praise. Everyone seemed to be an expert on how the schools should be managed. He discovered this when he served on the local school board. He really liked the high school principal and would chat with him on a regular basis when he came in to pick up the school mail. The principal's car was the first on campus in the morning and the last to leave at the end of the day. He did just about everything around the school. On Friday nights in the fall, he would manage the football ticket sales and make sure that the proceeds were secured before heading back to the parking lot to make sure that people left the premises in a safe manner. His job was never ending. I would see him in the hallways during class change and in the cafeteria during lunch. But never did I see him in one of my classrooms. He was too busy managing all of the things that a principal was expected to do.

Not much has changed for school principals. In spite of numerous studies and recommendations from a variety of professional organizations and universities (O'Neill, Fry, Hill & Bottoms, 2003; Hess & Kelly, 2005), the job continues to be overloaded with managerial tasks and administrivia. Finding time to visit classrooms and collaborate with teachers continues to be at a premium for most principals. Understanding how we got into this dilemma is important to know because it will help you let go of those things that are less important, so that you can transform your leadership and improve results.

Sorry, We Gave You the Wrong Directions

Many of us have waited until the evening before a birthday to put together a bicycle or a special toy, only to find that the box contained the wrong directions or none at all. This is exactly what we have done to principals. Today's principals are expected to lead schools in the improvement of the academic results of students. Yet on close examination of their job descriptions, principals are required to perform the majority of their work in areas that will not achieve the desired results. In a recent study of over 150 job descriptions of principals from rural, urban, and suburban schools in Texas, my research teams found that well over 80 percent of the responsibilities listed were unrelated to instructional leadership (Berkey, 2008a). In other words, principals have been handed the wrong set of directions to improve teaching and learning on their campuses.

We Also Gave You the Wrong Tool Belt

In the spring of 2003, Arthur Levine, former President of Teachers College at Columbia University, issued a report of a four-year study of principal and superintendent preparation programs offered by universities throughout the United States. The results were quite troubling. The study revealed that the majority of programs in school leadership were "inadequate to appalling." The content of courses was found to range from irrelevant to inadequate and the qualifications of the professors were limited in terms of actual field experience. Subsequent to the Levine report a number of other studies have examined principal preparation programs and have concluded that we need to retool the content and processes used to train people for the principalship (Bellamy, Fulmer, Murphy, & Muth, 2007; Davis, Darling-Hammond, LaPointe, & Meyerson, 2005; Hess & Kelly, 2005).

And Finally, We Couldn't Say No

Not only did we fail to provide principals with the right type of training and a clear set of expectations, we failed to say no to a plethora of programs and services that, over the course of the last 30 years, has overwhelmed schools and principals with extra work, much of which has little to do with schooling. Iowa businessman Jamie Vollmer (1994) told communities that schools were never meant to be a place where parents could drop off a kindergartner and years later pick up a fully developed adult. He made the case that as American society encountered new issues, it turned to the public schools instead of families to place fixes on the problems. Over the years, schools have taken on the roles of parents by teaching sex education, drug education, physical fitness, AIDS education, family abuse prevention, and many others areas of concern. Unfortunately, a variety of research shows that these programs don't improve the academic performance of children, and in many cases fail to have an impact on the societal problem they were designed to address (Santelli, Ott, Lyon, Rogers, Summers, & Schleifer, 2006; Brown & Brown, 2005; General Accounting Office, 2003; Cumming, Goulding, & Baggley, 1969). In reality many of these programs were created to make parents and community members feel that something was being done. School leaders couldn't say no and, as a result, we overwhelmed schools and principals at a time when their attention needed to be highly focused on teaching and learning.

The Good News: You Can Get Results by Changing Your Leadership

The road to improved student achievement is well marked. Parents have the greatest influence, but once children step onto a campus the teacher to whom they are assigned is the most important determinant, followed by the leader of the school. But the degree to which principals can influence student achievement will be measured by where and how they spend their time (Berkey, 2008c). Several studies have confirmed that, as principals devote more of their workdays to classroom visitations, collaboration with teachers, and leading improved learning initiatives, their influence on student achievement begins to expand (Wallace Foundation, 2006; Waters & Grub, 2004; and Waters, Marzano, & McNulty, 2003). Leadership counts when it comes to improving student achievement.

Getting Back to Learning

One of the impediments to improving the impact of principals on teaching and learning is their discomfort with the notion of instructional leadership. Keeping in mind that many principals were not trained to lead collaborative work in curriculum, instruction, and assessment, it goes without saying that they must build their knowledge and familiarity with the tools of the classroom. Throughout my experiences I have witnessed principals and superintendents who attempted to lead teachers without a solid understanding of the craft. This led to a gap in their credibility and ability to influence change. You don't have to be an expert, but you must demonstrate that you are learning and able to engage in thoughtful discussions about the classroom. Gone are the days when an administrator can use a checklist and be happy about seeing a tidy and orderly classroom. Effective principals have a deep understanding of the complexity of the learning processes, and how teachers must continuously collaborate to ensure that good academic growth is experienced by all children. This requires ongoing professional development and a heavy investment in daily work with teachers.

Taking Stock

In this chapter we examined how the economic and educational landscape has changed in America, and why school leaders must not only understand these issues, but more importantly, convey them to staff on a regular basis. One of the leading causes of ineffective school reform measures has been the inability of leaders to connect people with the purpose of change. Effective school leaders not only articulate the need for change, they model it through their actions. In the following chapter we will examine a process to help school principals take stock in their own leadership and alter their behaviors in ways to more effectively bring about improvements to their schools.

Chapter 2

The Path to Effective School Leadership

Be the change you want to see in the world.

—MAHATMA GANDHI

Effective leaders understand that in order to improve an organization, you must begin with reflecting on your own leadership and be willing to change. Each day represents an opportunity to prioritize those areas that will get your attention, and those that will not. To change the emphasis of your leadership, you must reorder your priorities, while also making sure that the organization is not disrupted by spending less time in areas that move down your list. The challenge in doing this is to break old habits and establish new ones by creating a rhythm to how you invest each day. This chapter will provide you with an overview of processes that will be expanded upon throughout the remainder of the book. The first process, covered in chapters 3–8, will describe the tools and techniques to assist you in identifying your present leadership practices, analyzing them in terms of effectiveness, and strategizing ways to reduce daily time in areas that don't count in order to increase time in areas that do. The second process, presented in chapters 9–15, will provide a framework of effective practices that principals can employ on a daily basis in order to have a greater impact on teaching and learning. Each component of the framework will be covered in detail, along with a planning and implementation process to transform daily work and scale up effectiveness.

Part I—
Altering Daily Practices:
The Principal as Leader of Best Practices

Knowledge management is the skill of getting best practice information to key people so that improvements can be acted upon and realized. In their book, *If Only We Knew What We Know*, Carla O'Dell and Jack Grayson (1998) revealed the power that organizations can tap by mastering the transfer of knowledge and best practices from one unit to another. Effective school leaders understand this and invest their time in the design of structures and processes that transfer knowledge and skills among teachers for the purpose of taking immediate actions to improve student learning. Effective principals use their technical expertise to engage staff in troubleshooting, brainstorming, and ongoing monitoring of daily progress towards improvement. When new ideas, technologies, or concepts are available in their field, they look for ways to integrate these into the organization.

I submit to you that principals must become leaders of best practices and engage themselves in a highly focused set of habits that are radically different from the past. We have the knowledge of what works to improve leadership of teaching and learning, and what does not. The transformation that needs to take place is the transfer of this knowledge to school leadership and the implementation of effective practices. Such a transformation can't happen overnight. It can only be accomplished by first auditing how principals invest their time, analyzing which of those investments have little or no value to improving results, and identifying strategies to reduce time in these areas in order to free up time for the structures and processes that will bring about improved teaching and learning. Figure 2.1 provides an overview of the steps that will be used to alter daily work habits in order to find time to lead best practices.

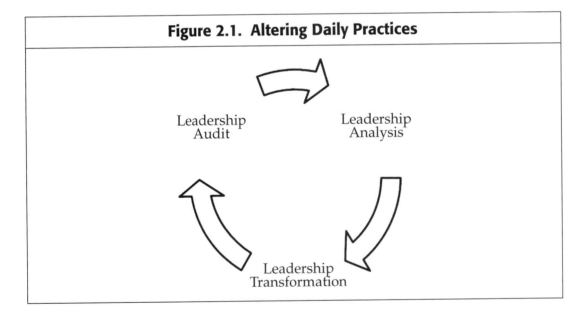

Figure 2.1. Altering Daily Practices

Leadership Audit

Leadership Analysis

Leadership Transformation

The Leadership Audit

When you begin a weight loss program, you not only get on the scales but also examine your daily habits and analyze these in relationship to factors that are key to bringing about desired results. Weight loss is all about changing behaviors, and in order to do so you have to take a deep breath and get very honest with yourself. The Leadership Audit works much the same way. The process involves keeping an accurate record of how you conduct your work throughout the day. Researchers have attempted to study principals using a variety of data collection techniques and some of these are quite involved and burdensome. The process I will share with you will be less cumbersome and fairly easy to use. The goal is to record a representative set of data that reflects how you spend your leadership time each day. You will utilize several sources of data to build an accurate profile of your leadership. And just like the beginning of a diet, you have to find the courage to stand in front a mirror and come to grips with the condition of your leadership. Once you have conducted the audit, you will be ready to analyze the data and begin the process of identifying those things that should move down your list of priorities and those that are more closely aligned to the work of a leader of best practices.

The Leadership Analysis

The Leadership Analysis is your moment of truth. While many principals suspect that they spend too much time conducting administrivia and tasks that are managerial in nature, my experience in using this tool is that principals are surprised, disappointed, embarrassed, and frustrated. This is normal. It's like seeing a picture of yourself when you were carrying a few extra pounds. The analysis is a critical part of the process because it will accomplish two things. First, it will help you get a real sense that how you spend your time represents what you feel is important, whether intentional or not. Your work defines your leadership. Second, it will help you begin the process of sorting out those areas that contribute to your instructional leadership and those that do not.

Once you have collected a list of the areas that typically consume your work day, it is important to analyze each one in relationship to the value added to improved teaching and learning. We will do this by using a rubric that helps you think about the degrees of these relationships. While not a perfect science, this process will give you a good picture of the present condition of your leadership practices.

The Leadership Transformation

Transforming your leadership is not an event that will happen over night. The best way to look at this is to realize that your present work habits developed over a period of time and became well-established routines and practices. Changing these will require you to develop a thoughtful plan that can be accomplished in stages with small gains spread over time.

The Leadership Transformation will take you through a methodical process of determining what to do with each of the tasks that you analyzed from your audit. Part of the process will require you to make a decision to eliminate, restructure, reassign, or enhance each work habit within the context of transforming your leadership. As each decision is made, you will develop strategies to facilitate the changes in your leadership behavior that coincide with the improvements you want to make in your daily practices.

Hundreds of graduate interns and principals have gone through this process, and I will share a few of their strategies to help you jump start your plan. Some of these will look viable, others will not, given your situation. I must caution that principals must develop strategies within the context of their present work setting. Every school has a unique set of conditions and culture that needs to be taken into consideration as a plan is developed. For example, we all know that a safe and orderly school campus is necessary to support the teaching and learning process. Some schools have established a culture whereby every adult takes considerable ownership in maintaining high expectations for order and discipline. In this situation, the time required of the principal is marginal because ownership has been established throughout the organization. In other school cultures there has been a heavy reliance on administration to be the primary provider of establishing order. These types of differences will guide the customization of your plan.

Practice, Practice, Practice

Notice that the process of auditing, analyzing, and transforming leadership practices is presented as a continuous cycle (Figure 2.1). Altering your daily habits will require a sustained approach and lots of practice using the cycle. Mistakes will be made and strategies will require periodic adjustments. In later chapters, we will examine how to use the cycle within a goal-setting process that will support your work and reduce time in areas that are less effective. For now, we will simply take a look at how it works.

Part II—
Spending Time on What Really Counts:
The Effective Principal Tracker

As you begin to implement a leadership transformation, you will free up time to invest in leadership practices that will improve the day-to-day performance of the organization. To acquaint you with these practices, I have developed a model that incorporates research findings from a variety of studies that have examined the type of work that principals should conduct in order to improve teaching and learning. These have been integrated with best practice leadership skills that come from the private sector, effective school research, and my own studies of school leadership. I have placed these into what I call a "Tracker," implying that it is important to re-route daily habits into the tracks that will make one's leadership more effective. The Effective Principal Tracker can be used as a framework for investing time in areas that will ensure results. Figure 2.2 displays the major components of the framework.

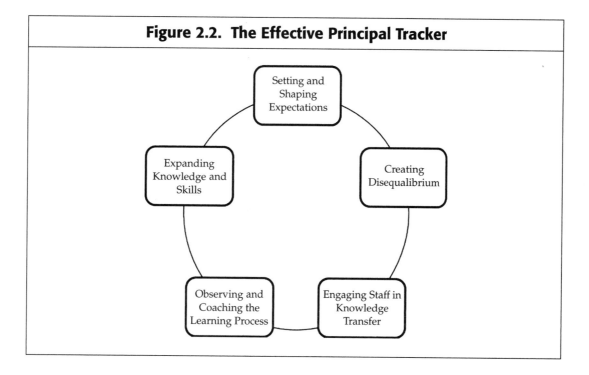

Figure 2.2. The Effective Principal Tracker

Setting and Shaping Expectations

As we examined in chapter 1, we need to make significant improvements to the education of our children in order to adequately prepare them for a fast-changing, competitive world. We also looked at the misapplication of strategic planning in school settings and how it leaves teachers confused and disconnected from the purpose and vision of the district. Principals can bring clarity to the vision of a school by engaging the faculty in a process that begins with the faculty responding to the following question:

What Do We Want Every Day, in Every Classroom, for Every Learner?

In order to respond to this question, principals and teachers must collaborate on a set of standards and expectations for the three critical elements of the learning process (see Figure 2.3).

All three of these elements require a careful and thoughtful study of best practices and transfer of knowledge among the staff. This approach empowers principals and teachers to focus the vision of the school through the lens of the classroom. Once the standards and expectations are in place, the culture of the school can take shape around the notion that leadership, resources, parents, and community should support the critical work of the classroom so that all children can succeed.

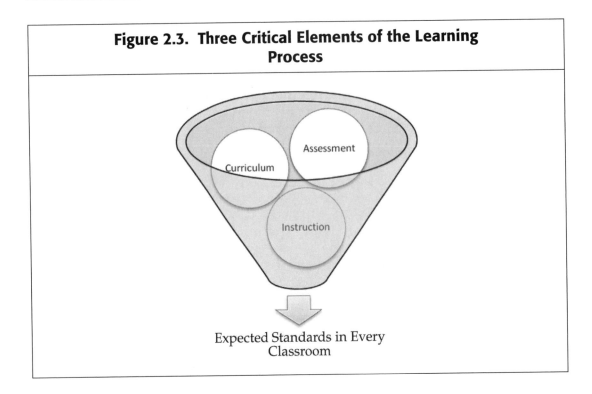

Figure 2.3. Three Critical Elements of the Learning Process

Curriculum

Assessment

Instruction

Expected Standards in Every Classroom

Creating Disequilibrium

Keeping things in balance will cause an organization to become complacent. Think about it. When the majority of adults are satisfied with the results, why change? If you want to improve, you must cause a change in the balance of your leadership by tipping the scales in favor of leadership versus management. This part of the Tracker will help you focus on your progress in transforming daily leadership to get results. It will also include ways to manage the change process as you engage others in their own change and improvement endeavors.

Engaging Staff in Knowledge Transfer

Principals are under pressure to improve the academic performance of their schools, and the best way to accomplish this is to bring teachers out of isolation and engage them in accessing and transferring knowledge among one another with the purpose of delivering improved learning for each student. As principals collaborate with teachers on the standards and expectations for curriculum, assessment, and instruction, and a sharpened vision is created, adults will realize that working together will make the job not only easier but much more effective. This requires an investment of the principal's time in creating structures that provide time for teachers to collaborate, helping them practice effective teamwork, and designing processes that will support knowledge transfer and best practice implementation. We will examine a variety of tools and techniques to build strong teams and intellectual capital among the teaching staff.

Observing and Coaching the Learning Process

For quite some time, principals have known that formal observation processes have limited impact on changing or improving teacher behaviors in the classroom. However, many have discovered that frequent informal visits, combined with the supportive coaching, can help teachers adjust and improve their instruction. Effective principals understand that through the supervision process the principal can provide one-on-one staff development (DuFour & Berkey, 1995). Classroom walk-throughs can be used for a variety of purposes in ways that open the door to collegial discussions and positive growth of instructional practices, if used appropriately. The Tracker will also include practices to ensure that students who experience learning difficulties can be identified early on and provided with support to reach mastery.

Expanding Knowledge and Skills

Transforming one's leadership does not have to be a lonely experience. In fact, I suggest and encourage principals to create their own learning team as they make changes to their leadership practices. Sharing failures and successes with colleagues makes a lot of sense and allows people to bounce ideas off one another. Principals find it difficult to continue their professional growth, and with new opportunities to do so, it is important to take advantage of this and get back into the mode of learning. This part of the Tracker will engage you in processes that will keep your instructional leadership skills sharpened through readings, reflection, professional training, and action research projects that bring energy and growth to your leadership.

Getting Started

We have learned that improving the effectiveness of one's leadership begins with an awareness of your current practices, and the skill sets that are closely aligned to those that influence improved teaching and learning. Getting started requires tools and structures to support the changes that you intend on making. Before you start a plan, it will be important to establish a baseline measurement of your leadership. You will also need to think about a support group, beginning with your superintendent or immediate supervisor. We will look at these strategies in the next two chapters.

Chapter 3

Building a Support Network for Leadership Transformation

Never doubt that a small group of thoughtful committed citizens can change the world. Indeed, it is the only thing that ever has.

—MARGARET MEAD

Changing the way you behave is very difficult if you attempt to do so without the understanding and support of those around you. In this chapter, we will take a look at two important components of an effective support network for your transformation plan. First, people need to understand why you are making a change. Helping them acquire a deep understanding of the purpose of your work will strengthen and enhance opportunities for conversations and relationship building, as they observe your new behaviors. Second, people need to feel connected to your efforts and how they will benefit from the transformation of your leadership. The strategies for accomplishing this will vary according to the roles and expectations that are linked between you and the individual(s).

Central Office

Having multiple conversations with the superintendent and central office supervisors is an essential starting point in making changes to your daily leadership. A stepping-off point for these discussions is the formal job description of the principal. If properly aligned, it should reflect what the school district expects the principal to achieve through the performance of specific responsibilities and associated behaviors. This is where disconnects take place and the focus on improved teaching and learning becomes blurred. For example, in a review of formal job descriptions of urban, suburban, and rural school principals, my research team identified that less than 20 percent of the responsibilities listed had any direct connection to leadership practices that influence student achievement (Berkey, 2008a). In many cases, principals were being evaluated on the basis of job descriptions that locked them into traditional roles. In addition, many central office administrators were trained to perform these same roles and thus expect the similar behaviors from their principals. However, for many principals, reality sets in when the state testing results for the school year are released and they suddenly find themselves being evaluated on the status of student achievement rather than a job description. This dilemma provides an important opportunity to shift the conversation to the following areas:

Q Why are you making the change?
A To improve the academic progress of each child by investing more time in daily leadership practices known to improve teaching and learning.

Q How will central office feel connected to the change and how will it benefit the district?
A Connections:
  1. Through involvement in realignment of the expected roles and responsibilities of the principal's job description with leadership practices that improve teaching and learning.
  2. Through involvement in feedback to the principal throughout the implementation of the practices.
  3. Through periodic reports from the principal on the progress of the implementation.

Benefits:
  1. Improved teaching and learning on the campus.
  2. The development of a new job description that could serve as a model for other administrative job descriptions in the district.
  3. The implementation of a pilot that could be studied by the district and extended to other campuses in the future.

The Principal's Job Description

Preparing a revised job description can be a good opportunity to engage central office in a thoughtful review of the literature and a team approach to revising the expectations of the principalship. Depending on the school district, major changes can be made all at once, while other settings may require a series of changes over time with gradual modifications. Appendix A illustrates a principal's job description based on the Effective Principal Tracker introduced in this book. It contains responsibilities and behaviors that highly connect with leadership practices that improve teaching and learning in schools. It also reflects significant changes to the role of the principal and requires considerable support from central office. Notice that the traditional responsibilities of the principal are listed as secondary to the leadership expectations. This is not to say that the principal no longer is responsible for these areas. Rather, it recognizes that the principal should not devote personal time to the delivery of these duties and tasks, but instead, oversee those who should.

Appendix B illustrates a job description reflective of the new standards for the preparation of school leaders by the National Policy Board for Educational Administration, the ISLLC standards. The job description reflects my personal attempt to translate the ISLLC standards into a formal job description. You will notice that the standards are a blend of instructional leadership along with traditional expectations of school leaders. While the standards represent a significant improvement over existing expectations found on principal job descriptions, they represent a more gradual shift that would be better suited for schools not ready for dramatic changes in leadership. Both examples have their own pluses and minuses and therefore I recommend using them only as a resource in customizing your own. If central office personnel are resistant to any changes to the formal job description, consider drafting one that would be considered a pilot document to be used and evaluated as you make changes to your leadership.

Working with central office to change the formal expectations of the principalship is just a starting point in gathering the support from those to whom you report. What follows is even more essential to your success. Remember that good communication with central office is proactive, and many times prevents people from being blindsided. Think about how and when you will keep them up to date on your transformation, so that their support remains a constant. As you discuss changes to your leadership behavior it is also important to identify roadblocks, challenges, and concerns and engage central office staff in an ongoing dialogue. It has been my experience that once a supervisor understands why you want to make a change, it provides a good foundation for mutual learning and support. Central office will also have concerns about how traditional responsibilities will be taken care of under a new plan. Involving them in the development of strategies will build ownership in the implementation. Later in the book we will examine specific strategies, but for now it is important to think about how you will bring central office administration into your plan.

Teachers

Collecting the support of teachers will likely be one of the most challenging issues in your transformation plan. First, as you change daily practices, teachers will see you more frequently in their classrooms and engaged in the improvement of teaching and learning. This can be intimidating. Second, teachers and principals have a longstanding tradition of working in isolation of each other. We tend to leave each other alone. Working together to achieve better results will be a cultural change for many schools. Before doing this it is important to have conversations with teachers that underscore the need for improved teaching and learning and leadership's role in supporting these endeavors. Give them the opportunity to provide you with feedback. Engage them in the review of your job description and allow them to discuss the role of the principal. Ask them to participate in evaluating your progress as you change daily habits.

For now, it is important to think about how you will convey the need to move away from managerial tasks and spend more time leading improved teaching and learning throughout the campus. The conversation should provide answers that teachers will want to know:

Q **Why you are making the change?**
A To improve my leadership by spending more time working with teachers on improvements to curriculum, instruction, and assessment.
Q **How teachers will feel connected to the change and how will it benefit them?**
A Connections:
1. Through involvement in the realignment of the principal's job description with practices that are known to provide teachers with stronger support, in the improvement of learning for every student.
2. Through involvement in feedback to the principal throughout the implementation of the practices.
3. Through greater contact with the principal in order to collaborate on important decisions that impact teaching and learning.
Benefits:
1. Greater support from the principal for teaching and learning.
2. Greater participation in decisions that impact teaching and learning.
3. Greater empathy from the principal, on the challenges of improving learning for every student.

Increased Visibility of the Principal

A natural consequence of investing more time in the teaching and learning process will be increased visits to the classroom and meetings with staff. This will be of concern to teachers unless there is a clear understanding of the purpose of the visits and meetings along with the intended consequences. Presented in the right way, it can be a significant opportunity for the principal to play the role of the learner and display a sincere interest in acquiring a deeper understanding of the challenges of the classroom. It is also an opportunity to distribute leadership as teachers gain more access to the principal and engage in collaborative work.

Support Staff

The support staff can be of great assistance in facilitating the changes that the principal is about to make. Having a conversation with custodial, secretarial, food service and other support staff on the need to improve teaching and learning can position these individuals to feel like they are making an important contribution in supporting the principal, teachers, and students. Calling on their leadership and asking for input on ways to help the principal spend more time with teachers and students, will strengthen their sense of ownership and importance to the mission of the school.

Some would point out that there is nothing wrong with the principal pushing a broom, checking restrooms, managing cafeteria lines, or preparing reports because it represents servant leadership. I suggest that this is a misinterpretation. Servant leadership calls for leaders to never think that there is a job too menial for them to perform. But it does not suggest that leaders spend valuable time conducting these tasks on a regular basis. Rather, it represents an opportunity for the leader to demonstrate empathy for support staff and empower them to take on a larger role of leadership in the performance of their work. In other words, as principals step away from performing routine managerial tasks, it can be turned into a win-win change by giving support staff the authority to fulfill responsibilities in a manner that gives them a greater amount of respect and self-confidence.

Q **Why are you making the change?**
A To spend more of my workday with teachers and students in order to improve learning.
Q **How will support staff feel connected to the change and how will it benefit them?**
A Connections:
1. Through involvement in the examination of the principal's job description to identify areas in which the support staff can participate.
2. Through involvement in feedback to the principal throughout the implementation of the transformation plan.
3. Through greater contact with the principal in order to collaborate on important decisions that impact the management of campus services.
Benefits:
1. Greater empowerment of support staff to manage campus services.
2. Greater participation in decisions that impact support staff.
3. Greater empathy from the principal on the challenges of managing the services provided to the campus.

The Old Job Description

Providing the support staff with the unrevised copy of the principal's job description can open the door to a frank discussion about authority and responsibility. Most people want to feel important and valued, and one of the ways to do this is to distribute leadership. Many of the traditional responsibilities that reside on a principal's job description can serve as a catalyst for people to talk about ideas and strategies that will decrease the principal's involvement and increase the staff member's leadership. Here is a short list of typical items that are found on principal job descriptions:

♦ Maintaining a safe and orderly environment
♦ Keeping an accurate inventory of supplies and equipment
♦ Overseeing the cleaning and maintenance of campus
♦ Scheduling and managing safety drills
♦ Resolving transportation problems for students
♦ Budgeting for the operational needs of the campus

Giving the support staff an opportunity to talk about these areas and providing them with the authority to act will raise their level of job satisfaction, and save the principal valuable time for work with teachers and students.

The Principal's Secretary

It has been my experience that secretaries typically want to please their boss, solve problems, and feel empowered to manage in the absence of the principal. These qualities are highly conducive to helping the principal reduce time in managerial tasks and get out of the office. With a minimal amount of training, collaboration, and follow-through, principals can engage their secretaries in becoming key supporters for the changes about to take place. Start with a conversation about the purpose of the changes and how essential it is to spend the majority of the workday out in the building, working with teachers and students.

One of the greatest concerns of the secretary will be how to find the principal in the event of an emergency and when to interrupt meetings and classroom visitations. It is important that the secretary feels empowered to do so, and therefore it is essential to develop guidelines and common understandings that will create a level of comfort. Another concern will be telephone calls from central office, parents, and others while the principal is out of the office. Helping the secretary understand how to communicate under these conditions will, in turn, provide empowerment, and a source of support for the transformation plan.

Q Why are you making the change?
A To spend more of my workday with teachers and students in order to improve learning.
Q How will the principal's secretary (or secretarial staff) feel connected to the change and how will it benefit her (them)?
A Connections:
   1. Through involvement in the examination of the principal's job description to identify areas in which the principal's secretary can participate.
   2. Through involvement in feedback to the principal throughout the implementation of the transformation plan.

3. Through greater consultation with the principal in order to collaborate on important decisions that will be shared with the principal's secretary.

Benefits:

1. Greater empowerment of the principal's secretary to provide administrative support.
2. Greater participation in decisions that impact the office of the principal.
3. Greater opportunity to fix problems that save time for the principal's secretary.

The Secretary's Job Description

There is no question that the principal's secretary is one of the most important individuals in the process of reprioritizing the daily work of the principal. While many secretaries are capable of handling work that carries higher levels of responsibility, most of them already have a full plate of duties. Thus, it is helpful to examine the job description of the principal's secretary at the same time the principal's job description is changing. The discussion should revolve around two questions:

1. What are the low-level tasks that consume the time of the principal's secretary?
2. What are the high-level tasks that consume the time of the principal that could be shared?

How does the Principal help the secretary offload low-level tasks? Many principals have employed a combination of parent volunteers and underutilized staff to pick up these tasks. In other situations, principals have discovered that their secretaries have taken on additional work because of their willingness to do things for teachers and staff. For example, in many schools, teachers ask the secretaries to complete purchase requisition forms that are unfamiliar to them. The list of "passed along" duties can be considerable and with some additional training of staff, it is possible to reduce these burdens and get everyone to take care of their own responsibilities.

Finally, some principals have elevated the position of the principal's secretary to one that more closely resembles an administrative assistant. While this is most likely a central office issue, it is worth exploring as a possible change in title as well as elevation on the pay scale. If this is not possible, principals will need to look to some alternative ways to reward their secretaries for being important partners in this work.

Parents

Parents have far less contact with the school principal than teachers and other staff. Their perceptions of the principal are formed through word of mouth, seeing the principal at school events and receiving occasional communications, such as newsletters and special messages. Thus, the changes that parents will notice as the principal spends more daily time in leading improvement in teaching and learning will be subtle. However, it can also become an issue if parents are accustomed to calling or e-mailing the principal and getting a quick response. If a principal spends a lot of the workday in the office, it is likely that parents have expected easy access whenever a question or problem arises. This can be handled proactively with some effective strategies that address communication. Equally important, principals will need to talk about their changing roles with key leaders and opinion shapers among the parent community. It would be helpful to invite PTA representatives and other parents who are highly involved in the school to informal meetings and conversations about the importance of leading improved teaching and learning:

Q **Why are you making the change?**
A To spend more of my workday in classrooms with teachers and students in order to ensure quality learning for all children.

Q **How will the parents feel connected to the change and how will it benefit them?**
A Connections
  1. Through involvement with the principal in discussions about improving the academic success of their students.
  2. Through involvement in feedback to the principal on the quality of their child's learning experiences and achievement.
  3. Through greater consultation with the principal in order to collaborate on ways to help parents support the improvement of their child's learning.
Benefits:
  1. Greater attention to their child's academic progress and success.
  2. Greater participation in decisions that impact their child's learning.
  3. Greater opportunity to fix problems when their child is not learning.

Accessibility to the Principal

Parent support is critical and the issue of accessibility to the principal is one that will need much attention. Having an open discussion with a representative group of parents can be useful in identifying ways to ensure that parents maintain open access to the principal, but in ways that reflect the priorities of the school. Most parents are reasonable and will support changes if you engage them in collaborative planning, so that their issues are addressed. The following questions are ones that will be important to consider in the identification of strategies to maintain adequate parent access to the principal:

  1. Under what circumstances is it reasonable to contact the principal directly about an issue or problem?

2. What are the reasonable expectations in terms of the promptness of a reply from the principal?

While such a discussion and formulation of strategies will not resolve all potential issues, it will provide key parent leaders with assurance that the principal will use their advice and suggestions as a roadmap for maintaining open access for parents with concerns. Keep in mind that parents want their children to be successful and improving the effectiveness of teaching and the academic progress of their students is job one.

Linking the Support System with Objective Feedback

In this chapter we examined the importance of establishing your support system and engaging key people. Members of the school family need to know why you are changing the emphasis of your leadership, how it will impact them, and how they can become critical partners in making it all happen. However, this is only the beginning of gathering important input from support system members. In the next chapter we will take a look at the use of feedback instruments that will allow individuals to give the principal anonymous and objective information at various stages of the transformation.

Chapter 4

Measuring and Driving Your Transformation

Drive thy business, let not that drive thee.

—BENJAMIN FRANKLIN

In his book, *Good to Great*, Jim Collins (2001) described good-to-great leaders as "...a study in duality: modest and willful, humble and fearless (p. 22)." The first part of this chapter will examine ways to establish a baseline measurement of your leadership using instruments and processes that provide important feedback both in the short run and over a substantial period of time. This is important for two reasons. First, effective leaders learn how to hold their egos in check and listen to vital feedback from others regarding their leadership. Second, studies of human behavior (Sarafino, 2001) tell us that changes can be sustained if positive reinforcement is introduced at various intervals. Inserting checkpoints throughout your transformation will provide the synergy to keep your progress moving forward. The later part of this chapter will be devoted to a means of building passion. Passion is the engine that drives change, and by tapping your personal sense of moral purpose, you will find the strength to change your leadership with courage and intention.

360° Assessments

An Objective View of Reality

Peter Senge (1990) tells us that a core component of achieving personal mastery is the ability to examine reality with a high level of objectivity. Therefore, if we are to grow and sustain our capacity to lead others, it is important to first start with a close examination of the present conditions of our leadership. There are good tools to accomplish this. One of the most effective is the use of a 360° assessment that paints an overall picture of one's leadership, yet also provides useful feedback for reaching higher levels of mastery.

Types of 360° Leadership Assessments

Three-hundred-sixty-degree assessments are designed to provide a measurement of how people in an organization perceive a person's performance, based on a set of criteria. In our case, we want feedback on our leadership skills. The typical process involves a self-evaluation combined with assessments conducted by employees, peers, and supervisors. The person being evaluated selects people who will provide honest and fair feedback. The results are tallied and provided only to the person under assessment. The purpose of the 360° is to give individuals important information about themselves and is not intended to serve as part of a formal performance evaluation. Rather, it offers a set of data that can be used to strengthen the professional development of the individual.

While there are a variety of 360° assessments in existence, we will review three that I believe are worthy of consideration in helping establish a baseline measurement of leadership. Two are from the field of education, and the third is from the private sector. All are well-established instruments with good reliability and validity. Each is available as an online assessment that makes it easier to administer and use. Additional information can be obtained at the respective websites for each assessment listed in the reference section under the corresponding authors.

NASSP Leadership Skills Assessment

The National Association of Secondary School Principals (NASSP, 2008) has developed a five-step *Leadership Skills Assessment* that provides a diagnosis of important skills sets in leading elementary, middle level, or high schools. The instrument can be used by up to 15 people to measure their perception of how the leader performs ten skill dimensions covering four areas of leadership:

Instructional Leadership
    Setting instructional direction
    Teamwork
    Sensitivity
Resolving Complex Problems
    Judgment
    Results orientation
    Organizational ability
Communication
    Oral communication
    Written communication
Developing Self and Others
    Understanding own strengths and weaknesses
    Developing others

The leader can select the individuals to participate and all responses are recorded anonymously. Additional features of this assessment include an in-basket activity to assess the leader's performance in dealing with a variety of issues, and follow-up reports to provide feedback and planning processes to build professional skills.

Balanced Leadership Profile

Based on the Mid-Continent Regional Education Laboratory (McREL) model of balanced leadership, the profile is designed to provide a principal with multiple perspectives on the delivery of 21 leadership responsibilities correlated to the improvement of student achievement (Waters, Marzano, & McNulty, 2005). Another interesting feature of the profile is that it provides an indication if the initiative being led by the principal is a *first-order change* (e.g., consistent with present norms, practices, or knowledge) or *second-order change* (e.g., a break from past and requiring new knowledge and skills).

McREL 21 Leadership Responsibilities	
1. Culture	11. Outreach
2. Order	12. Input
3. Discipline	13. Affirmation
4. Resources	14. Relationships
5. Curriculum, instruction, assessment	15. Change agent
6. Focus	16. Optimizer
7. Knowledge of curriculum, instruction, assessment	17. Ideals/beliefs
	18. Monitors/evaluates
8. Visibility	19. Flexibility
9. Contingent rewards	20. Situational awareness
10. Communication	21. Intellectual simulation

The survey requires a minimum of five teachers to participate along with a supervisor. All feedback is anonymous and confidential. The report provides information on the strengths and areas for improvement of the leader. In addition, it identifies next steps to be taken with the initiative being led. The website for the assessment offers a variety of resources that support improvement in each of the 21 responsibilities as well as the management of change.

Leadership Practices Inventory

Perhaps the most widely used leadership instrument in existence, the *Leadership Practices Inventory* (LPI), comes from the work of Jim Kouzes and Barry

Posner's *The Leadership Challenge* (1995). The 360° instrument is designed to measure the five practices and ten commitments of their Leadership Challenge Model:

Challenging the Process
1. Search out challenging opportunities to change, grow, innovate, and improve.
2. Experiment, take risks, and learn from accompanying mistakes.

Inspiring a Shared Vision
3. Envision an uplifting and ennobling future.
4. Enlist others in a common vision by appealing to their values, interests, hopes, and dreams.

Enabling Others to Act
5. Foster collaboration by promoting cooperative goals and building trust.
6. Strengthen people by giving power away, providing choice, developing competence, assigning critical tasks, and offering visible support.

Modeling the Way
7. Set the example by behaving in ways that are consistent with shared values.
8. Achieve small wins that promote consistent progress and build commitment.

Encouraging the Heart
9. Recognize individual contributions to the success of every project.
10. Celebrate team accomplishments regularly.

The instrument consists of 30 items and takes only 10–20 minutes to complete. The leader completes a self-inventory and selects 5–10 people to provide anonymous and confidential feedback. An online report is generated to assist the leader in examining strengths and areas for growth.

Timing and Frequency of the 360° Assessment

While the 360° can be administered at anytime, it is important to conduct the first assessment prior to embarking on any changes in your leadership practices. The optimum time to do this is toward the beginning of a school year, once the students and staff are into their work routines. This will also enable you to conduct a post-assessment prior to the end of the school year. Think of the 360° as a summative assessment in the sense that you are capturing a baseline measurement at the beginning, and one later on to determine the growth in mastery of your leadership skills.

Tools and Processes to Support Leadership Transformation

We know that when people want to lose weight, they must also have a means of measuring progress at intervals to first determine if their strategies are working, and second, to provide intermittent reinforcement to keep them motivated to achieve the goal. The same holds true for making substantive changes to your daily leadership. Thus, goal setting and attainment in short intervals will be an essential means of targeting your changes and measuring your progress throughout the school year.

Using SMART Goals to Improve Your Leadership Practices

Hundreds of variations of the use of SMART goals have been around for quite some time, and if used wisely and effectively, can contribute to the successful attainment of large changes in an individual, as well as an organization. Because so many people have used this process and are comfortable with it, I have found it useful to integrate SMART goals into the processes used in this book to shift leadership behaviors toward more effective practices.

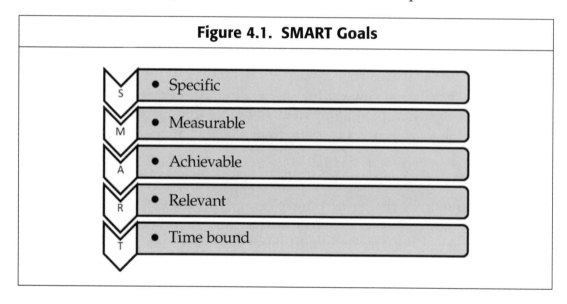

Figure 4.1. SMART Goals

- Specific
- Measurable
- Achievable
- Relevant
- Time bound

Specific

Principals can set specific goals that will help them reduce the amount of time devoted to tasks and responsibilities that consume large portions of their work day. Conversely, effective principals set goals for themselves that get them into classrooms on a regular basis and engage them in important instructional leadership. In order for the goal to be specific, principals must identify those strategies and behaviors that will improve their effectiveness. Key questions when addressing the specificity of a goal include:

What am I attempting to accomplish?
What are the concrete behaviors I am attempting to change?

We will use the SMART goal framework to establish and achieve goals in the following areas:

♦ Decreased use of daily time to perform managerial work
♦ Increased use of daily time in effective leadership practices

Measurable

Measurement is a critical component that enables the goal setter to see progress at various intervals along the way, as well as successful attainment at the end. Some fundamental measurement questions to ask when establishing a goal are:

How will I know when I have achieved the goal?
How can I measure the goal in simple ways that are not cumbersome?
How frequent should the measurements be in order to determine progress?

Measurement can be messy, especially if the desired outcomes are not specific enough to get a clear understanding of the changes that will take place. It is equally important to think about how the measurement will be recorded at frequent intervals without using considerable resources and time.

We will use SMART goals to:

♦ Set measurable benchmarks for changes in leadership behavior
♦ Organize benchmark attainment in ways that are easy to measure
♦ Provide ongoing progress reports to reinforce changes being made

Achievable

The goal should be challenging and cause the principal to stretch and grow. But it also should be reachable. Thus it will be important to consider how wide the gap is between the present condition of your leadership and the desired change you are identifying in the goal. Setting smaller, achievable goals will be more productive in sustaining change than selecting ones that are so large you lose interest, focus, and motivation. Consider the following questions:

Is the goal realistic considering my present skill sets and abilities?
Is the goal challenging enough to cause me to stretch and grow?
Is the goal attainable within a reasonable amount of time?

SMART goals will keep your plan achievable by:

♦ Setting incremental benchmarks that denote progressive change
♦ Providing just enough stretch that promotes change
♦ Aligning appropriate amounts of time with goal attainment

Relevant

A relevant goal should be highly congruent with the intentions of the goal setter. In this case, the goal should be tightly wrapped around the improvement of the principal's leadership skills and practices. Some important questions to consider are:

How does the goal improve my performance as a principal?
Do I have the capacity to achieve the goal?
Will others understand and support the pursuit of this goal?

Using SMART goals will ensure that the changes being made in your daily practices are relevant to the overriding goal of improving teaching and learning by:

♦ Matching the change in leadership behavior with those that impact teaching and learning
♦ Examining if you have the knowledge and skills to make the change
♦ Determining if you have engaged those around you in ways that help them understand and support the changes you are attempting to make

Time-bound

Goals must have a deadline. Without one there can be no commitment to achieving them. Timelines provide the necessary accountability to keep you focused on the important changes to your leadership. Keeping a completion date that is short will increase the likelihood that continuous progress will be made. It also facilitates the development of a schedule for intermittent measurements of goal completion. Essential questions to consider include:

Is the deadline realistic considering the goal to be achieved?
Does the length of time for goal achievement allow for intermittent measurement?
Who will enforce the deadline and how?

Not every goal will be achieved by the stated deadline. But in cases where they are not, it provides an opportunity to reflect and learn. SMART goals can ensure that the time allotted to the goal is finite by:

♦ Setting a realistic completion date
♦ Identifying intermittent dates for measuring progress to goal attainment
♦ Determining who will hold you accountable for the deadline and how this will take place.

In the second half of this book we will use the SMART goal process as a major component of your plan to improve effectiveness.

Using a 360° to assess the present condition of your leadership is an effective means of setting a baseline for the improvements you intend to make in your overall leadership of a school. It will prepare you for taking a closer look at your daily practices. It will also provide important information in setting goals to ratchet up those areas that will improve teaching and learning and scale down those that don't. Before moving onto the processes of auditing, analyzing, and transforming daily practices, we will turn to an important source of energy that can drive the changes you are about to make.

Passion as an Engine to Drive Your Leadership

We often assume that if we show people how to change, they will use the knowledge and skills presented to improve results. But as stated earlier, we quickly slide over the discussion of purpose. People resist change, especially if they are not heavily connected with a compelling reason to do so. Michael Fullan (2001) cautioned us that, "Whatever one's style, every leader, to be effective, must work on improving his or her moral purpose" (p. 13). In chapter 1 of this book we examined some of the looming issues that should cause all school leaders to ramp up the improvement of teaching and learning. There is no question that the race for economic supremacy cuts directly to the issue of moral purpose in our work. The examples of what our children will face in a globally competitive world should cause all educators to pause, and refocus their work with a high sense of urgency. Leaders don't have to look too far within their schools to find moral issues that will build passion for change and improvement. I offer the following story as an illustration of how the issue of inequity can be a driving passion behind a plan to improve your leadership.

A Moral Issue

In spite of considerable research on the drawbacks of tracking curriculums (Oakes, 1985), there are still a number of schools that sort and select children and place them into tracks or levels to best meet their needs. Every school I worked in employed various types of tracking. In some cases, it was used effectively to challenge advanced learners. But in others, it was apparent that students assigned to the lower levels not only failed to benefit, but were hurt academically. Such was the case in a school where students were placed into one of three tracks in language arts as they entered their freshman year.

Some of the most hurtful things we do to students start with a well intended purpose. When I asked teachers why the three-level system was created, they stated that it was designed to serve the academic needs of students by placing them according to their ability level. They were particularly proud of the lowest level, and to their credit, kept the average class size below that of the other two. Students in the lower level were taught the same objectives as the other levels, using instructional materials that were suited for their perceived abilities.

This all sounded good, but leaders have to dig deeper and confront the facts. I made a trip to the guidance office and read through the files of dozens of students, trying to understand how they were identified and placed into the lowest level. I also examined the grades that were assigned to students in all three levels, going back five years. Here is what my investigation revealed:

♦ Students were assigned to each of the three levels based on their achievement record (state assessment score, grades) as well as the teacher's impression of their performance (completion of homework, attendance, motivation level) in middle school. Thus, placement was determined by achievement level rather than ability.

♦ Had ability test scores been used, teachers would have discovered that many students were misplaced. Half of the lower ability students were assigned to one of the upper levels instead of the lowest. And about half of the students who were assigned to the lowest level should have been placed in upper levels.

♦ Students who were misplaced in the upper levels earned higher grades than those who were incorrectly placed in the lower level.

♦ Students who were placed in the lowest level were assigned twice the number of D's and F's than those in other levels.

♦ Upward or downward movement of students from one level to another rarely occurred as they moved through subsequent years.

Perhaps the most passionate reaction I had to all of this occurred when I interviewed seniors who spent their entire high school experience in the lowest level of language arts. These were students who presented attendance and discipline problems and had developed thick skins to protect themselves from the labels that had been placed on them. In the privacy of my office, several broke into tears when I asked why they were placed in lower classes and what they had learned from a program that was suppose to be customized to their needs. They felt embarrassed, humiliated, and abandoned.

The facts were overwhelming. We were hurting children and my immediate reaction was to disband the program immediately without discussion or collaboration. This would have been a mistake. Instead, leaders must use situations like these to not only heighten their sense of moral purpose, but as Fullan explained, develop it in others to cultivate relationships and create a common vision. It took many months to convince the staff to change this practice, but my passion and the passion I nurtured in others eventually enabled it to happen. Never underestimate the power of passion.

Get Passionate, Remain Passionate

Rick Warren (2008) wrote a best-selling book, *The Purpose Driven Life* and set of materials that caused people to reconnect with their faith and sense of purpose in their daily work. While I am not promoting his work to engage people in religious practice, I share his point that purpose should be the driving force behind one's daily actions. The purpose of improving one's leadership has a moral center. I believe all educators share a moral purpose in improving education for all children so that their lives will be happy and productive. A strong sense of moral purpose provides us with an important source of passion that can deliver the daily energy to transform our leadership and make a difference in the lives of our students. All schools face significant issues that connect with moral purpose. Here is a sample of some of the questions that we can raise to stir passion among ourselves and our staff:

- As we celebrate that 80% of our students reached proficiency on a state exam, what is our commitment to the other 20%?
- Should our commitment to students who come to school unprepared be the same as our commitment to those that do?
- If we concede that students learn at different rates, shouldn't we differentiate curriculum, instruction, and assessment accordingly?
- Other professions work collaboratively to meet the needs of their clients. Why do we allow people to work in isolation of one another?

Reactions to these questions generate passion and start a healthy conversation that focuses us on our sense of purpose. Passion is a powerful source that leaders must first tap within themselves, and in turn, grow in others in ways that reconnect people with their purpose. You can only reduce passion by choosing not to care or take action. Effective leaders confront the former and do the latter.

Next Steps

In this chapter we looked at how to measure the state of one's leadership before making changes to transform and improve the effectiveness of leadership practices. We also reviewed a goal-setting framework that will come in handy as we target areas for short-term gains and long-term success. Finally, we discussed how we can use a sense of moral purpose as an energy source that taps our passion and drives our daily work. In the next chapter we will begin the process of auditing daily habits and examining what gets the attention of the principal.

Chapter 5

The Leadership Audit

The perfection of one's self is the fundamental base of all progress and all moral development.

—CONFUCIUS

In the previous chapter we looked at the use of a 360° assessment to measure how you and those who work with you perceive the present state of your leadership. This is analogous to stepping on the scales and accepting the results. Yet, many weight loss experts will tell you that it is equally important to examine your behavior patterns in order to know what to change. Poor eating habits and sedentary lifestyles are difficult patterns to change. So are the habits that hold us back from improving the effectiveness of our leadership. In this chapter we will look at a process that will help you acquire a clearer understanding of how you spend your work day.

Purpose of the Audit

How much do you really know about your daily leadership practices? If you are like most principals, it may be easy to identify general areas that get your attention, but placing any specificity to these or analyzing how much time you devote to any particular practice can be challenging. A school principal's typical day is consumed by a whirlwind of activities, demands, issues, and challenges. No two days are alike, and this makes reflecting on one's practice a difficult endeavor to perform. The purpose of the Leadership Audit is to capture several snapshots of daily leadership practices in order to study your habits and make desired changes.

Be Honest with Yourself

While you won't get an exact measurement of how you distribute your time each day, it is important to capture an overall picture that represents a close approximation to reality. I remember a friend telling me how he eats healthy in the weeks leading up to his annual physical in hopes of keeping his cholesterol count down. The purpose of the leadership audit is to help yourself, not enable habits that hold you back. Your goal is not to make the audit look good, but rather to make sure it presents an accurate sketch of your typical work day.

The Content of the Audit

The audit involves the collection of two types of data:

1. Specific tasks performed throughout the workday (qualitative)
2. Time spent on each task (quantitative)

While you can record both of these simultaneously, it can be challenging to do so and therefore I recommend that you consider separating these for now. Identifying the specific tasks that consume your time will be the easier of the two sets of data to collect. The goal is to record as many different types of things that you do in order to facilitate an analysis of each one in the next step of the process. Many of these can be identified by simply starting with a blank paper and listing everything you remember. But it is also important to capture these data in a more direct and planned manner.

Collecting Qualitative Data of Tasks Performed

Qualitative data come from a variety of sources and provide the benefit of capturing a more complete picture of events. You can use a number of resources to accomplish this type of data collection:

Daily planner
Microsoft Outlook or other electronic calendar
Meeting agenda
PDA (personal digital assistant)
Electronic log

The more resources you employ, the more accurate your data will become. At the same time, the process should not be so cumbersome that it is too difficult to perform. Thus, we will start with what you already know about your work habits and fill in the holes by collecting data during specific times of the day. This will be accomplished in three steps:

1. Identify what you already know
2. Schedule and collect data
3. Complete the audit

Starting with the End in Mind

The qualitative data of the leadership audit should be a collection of identified tasks, practices, and responsibilities that fill up a typical day of work. In our study of principal and principal interns (Berkey, 2008b), we found these data clustered around common areas. In the beginning of our study we asked principals and principal interns to start with a blank sheet of paper and record all of the different work they performed throughout the day. As categories emerged from the data, we found it useful to develop an instrument that listed these areas in order to make it easier for the principal or observer to collect the data. Figure 5.1 on page 42 displays the instrument you will be using throughout the auditing process. It contains ten categories along with the option to add other categories depending on your circumstances. There are examples of practices for each of the categories in order to provide you with a frame of reference.

Provided below is a more complete description of each of the categories listed on the Leadership Audit form.

Safe and Orderly Environment   One of the most time consuming areas of responsibility for the principal is maintaining order and safety throughout the campus. Some of the daily work includes direct contact with students in the administration of attendance and discipline procedures, as well as the monitoring of hallways, parking lots, and common areas where people assemble. For principals who have assistants that perform much of this work, there are other responsibilities that can consume time. Principals hear discipline appeals, work on policy and procedures for student behavior, oversee campus security planning, and coordinate safety standards and procedures with local law enforcement and fire protection officials. A growing area of responsibility is the health risks of students. Principals coordinate nursing services and oversee the unique challenges of children with allergies, diseases, injuries, and mental health issues.

Fiscal Management   Principals are key players in the development and administration of the budget cycle in a school district. Responsibilities range from completing purchase orders to engaging faculty and staff in the preparation of budgetary needs for the coming school year. Principals also monitor fund balances and spend considerable time making adjustments to the implementation of the budget. In addition, principals also reported that they manage student activity accounts, grant funds, vending machine collections, and fundraising activities.

Communication   Communicating with students, parents, central office, and the community is a daunting responsibility for principals. On the receiving end, principals manage dozens of pieces of mail, numerous phone calls, and a growing plethora of e-mails with the expectation of a quick response. At the same time, principals attempt to be proactive with their communications by writing newsletters, memos to the staff and central office, and individual correspondence to parents and community. Of equal importance is establishing a positive relationship with the local news media and communicating the good news of the school.

Instructional Leadership   Leading instruction includes a broad set of responsibilities, including formal observations of teachers, post-conferences,

Figure 5.1. Leadership Audit		
Area	**Examples of Practices**	**Your Practices**
Safe and Orderly Environment	◆ Discipline ◆ Attendance ◆ Supervision of students ◆ Campus security ◆ Nursing and health services	
Fiscal Management	◆ Budgets ◆ Purchasing ◆ Fundraising ◆ Activity accounts ◆ Grant funds	
Communication	◆ E-mails ◆ Phone calls ◆ Memos ◆ Mail ◆ Newsletters ◆ News media ◆ Correspondence	
Instructional Leadership	◆ Observations ◆ Walk-throughs ◆ Data analysis ◆ Team meetings ◆ Curriculum work ◆ Teacher collaboration	
Event Supervision and Attendance	◆ Extracurricular events ◆ Athletics ◆ Music programs ◆ Recognition ceremonies	
Special Education and 504s	◆ Special education meetings ◆ Meetings with special ed. staff ◆ Review of IEPs ◆ 504 meetings ◆ Appeals ◆ Court proceedings	
Parents and Community	◆ Meetings ◆ PTA ◆ Booster club ◆ Open house ◆ Band parents ◆ Parent support groups ◆ Parent conferences ◆ Community groups	

(Cont'd.)

Figure 5.1. Leadership Audit *(Continued)*		
Area	**Examples of Practices**	**Your Practices**
Staff	◆ Personal issues ◆ Substitutes ◆ Faculty meetings ◆ Staff training ◆ Staff celebrations	
Facilities and Services	◆ Maintenance ◆ Custodial services ◆ Parking lot ◆ Transportation ◆ Food services ◆ Technology	
Administrivia	◆ Paperwork ◆ Test administration ◆ Room scheduling ◆ Report cards ◆ Central office meetings ◆ Master schedule	
Other		

classroom walk-throughs, curriculum management, and coordination of assessment and data systems. Linked to this, principals work with teachers to improve instruction through establishing and supporting communities of practice, collaborating on improvements to curriculum and assessments, and analyzing data to diagnose and resolve learning problems.

Event Supervision and Attendance Principals are expected to be seen at the majority of the events sponsored by the school. These include athletics, fine arts, clubs, special organizations, and recognition ceremonies. In many cases, principals act as supervisors of events and involve themselves in duties ranging from crowd control to collection of gate receipts.

Special Education and 504s Principals invest a considerable amount of time overseeing and engaging the processes in place to assure that all children with special needs receive an appropriate education in a least restrictive setting. Many principals sit in on every annual review meeting while others are involved in the specific design of the individual education plan for each student. Principals also engage in meetings with special education staff and special education students and parents. They spend time with appeals, court proceedings, and remedies for issues related to special education students. A growing area of responsibility for principals includes dealing with the unique needs of students that do not fall under special education but qualify for 504 services.

Parents and Community Meetings with parents take up significant amounts of the principal's time. Leading reasons for the meetings include attendance and discipline issues, academic problems, family issues, and special requests. In addition, principals plan and lead formal events that bring parents into the school such as open houses, parent nights, and orientations. Most schools have parent organizations and principals are asked to attend meetings, volunteer at functions, and coordinate school resources. The same can be true for community organizations that expect the principal to engage with them on a regular basis.

Staff Outside of the interactions with teachers to improve instruction and learning, principals invest time in familiarizing staff with policies and procedures, leading informational meetings, celebrating staff achievements, and assisting staff with administrative support. Many principals oversee the arrangements when a teacher is absent from work, including obtaining a substitute, checking in on substitutes, and following through on related paperwork. One of the surprising phenomena of the principalship is the volume of time devoted to counseling and supporting staff with personal problems.

Facilities and Services On most campuses, principals are the managers of many types of services to students and staff. These include custodial and maintenance, food, transportation, clerical, and technology. Although not directly involved in the provision of these services, many principals report that they spend considerable time monitoring these and troubleshooting related problems.

Administrivia Principals handle a large amount of paperwork and general administrative duties that fall under the category of administrivia. This category is provided as a catch all for the plethora of little tasks associated with a responsibility such as test administration, issuance of report cards, assignment of rooms, creation of a master schedule, preparing reports, and attending central office meetings. The range of tasks in this area include a wide variety of specific tasks that are special to certain campuses, such as raising and lowering the flag, to ones that are common among most principals, such as filing state reports.

Other Some principals have unique sets of responsibilities associated with their campus and thus a category is provided to capture this data. Another option is for principals to add special categories unique to their position. For example, principals of alternative schools, vocational schools, gifted academies, or Title I campuses have a large number of related duties that can be placed into a category that is unique to their setting. Other special features of a school can also cause the establishment of additional categories that consume the time of the principal.

Steps of the Audit

Step 1: Identify What You Already Know

The best source of the audit is you. Begin with your own perceptions of how you invest your daily time. Using the Leadership Audit instrument, list the daily practices that you consider to be part of your regular work routine. The examples listed next to each of the ten categories are there to trigger and stimulate your reflection, not to suggest what you actually do in practice. For example, let's say you are a principal of a large school with several assistants who handle the day to day attendance and discipline issues. Under the Safe and Orderly Environment category you might report less activity than a principal with no assistants. Your Leadership Audit might look like this:

Area	Examples of Practices	Your Daily Practices
Safe and Orderly Environment	♦ Discipline ♦ Attendance ♦ Supervision of students ♦ Campus security ♦ Nursing and health services	♦ Expulsions ♦ Suspension appeals ♦ Meetings with Assistant Principals to discuss campus issues

Or perhaps you are a principal who just took a principalship in a school that is experiencing a considerable number of disciplinary issues, and you are understaffed with only one assistant principal. Your audit could look quite different for this category:

Area	Examples of Practices	Your Daily Practices
Safe and Orderly Environment	♦ Discipline ♦ Attendance ♦ Supervision of students ♦ Campus security ♦ Nursing and health services	♦ Supervision of student arrival/dismissal ♦ Lunchroom supervision ♦ Discipline hearings ♦ Management of attendance ♦ Removal of students ♦ Supervision of hallways and restrooms ♦ Duty schedules

As you work through your first listing using the Leadership Audit, keep in mind that there is no special magic to each of the categories. They are presented only as a means of clustering your data. Feel free to create your own categories as needed. Some of this is due to the setting and culture of the school, the specific job description of the principal, and the personal preferences of the individual. After completing the first draft, put the audit aside for a day or two and come back to it for further revisions. Once you feel comfortable with your initial audit, it is time to move on to step 2.

Step 2: Schedule and Collect Data

Unless you are the exception to the rule, there are many duties and tasks that principals perform that don't immediately come to mind when asked to list them in an audit. Thus, it is important to fill in the gaps by collecting some qualitative data in the work setting at different times during the week. The following process will minimize disruption to your workday, yet yield valuable information about your work habits.

The 2 + 2 + 2 Approach

This formula allows you to schedule your data collection over two weeks, using four half-day time frames with two in the morning hours, and two in the afternoon:

- ♦ Two mornings
- ♦ Two afternoons
- ♦ Within two weeks

Using half-day collection periods makes it more manageable to focus on recording accurate data. It also allows you to strategically place these according to your calendar and your work habits. Try to place two of the collection points at your least productive times and two at your most productive times. Principals report that, on average, their Mondays and Fridays are less productive than the middle days of the week. A typical schedule for data collection would look like this:

		Monday	Tuesday	Wednesday	Thursday	Friday
Week 1	AM	X		X		
Week 2	PM		X			X

How to Collect the Data

This step is not intended to be an intense data collection process, but rather a capture of qualitative data that represent how you spend your time during a morning or afternoon of a typical work day. For that reason, use whatever methodology that works best for you. If you have a pretty good short term memory, it might be easy for you to simply use a blank copy of the Leadership Audit instrument and take the last 20 minutes of your morning or afternoon to reconstruct how you spent your time. Another option is to keep the instrument close by and make notes throughout the audit session. Some principals use personal digital assistants (PDAs), daily planners or calendars to schedule appointments, meetings, and priorities. If you do, you might use one of these tools and spend a little more attention to detail during the audit. If none of these techniques work for you, simply jotting down anecdotal notes on a pad can work just as well. Consider experimenting with a different collection technique for each of the four sessions. Again, don't make it cumbersome and do what comes most natural to you.

Step 3: Fill in the Gaps

Pull your original draft of the Leadership Audit and use your data from Step 2 to add more items under each of the categories. You can also add more categories if you notice a cluster of related activities that consumed your workday. This is a good time to reflect on your work during the past two weeks and add more items, even though they didn't occur during one of the four audit sessions. Once you have your final draft, put it in a safe place for use during the Leadership Analysis process covered in the next chapter.

Conducting a Quantitative Time Audit

Most of the studies of how principals conducted their work included some type of time audit. The purpose is to quantify the distribution of time in order to assess what areas get the most and least amount of attention. Some of the techniques are quite sophisticated, using electronic devices that signal the principal to record data at random times throughout the day. Other processes employ the use of an observer who records information at regular intervals such as every 15 minutes. I have kept this type of audit separate from our qualitative collection for several reasons. First, the time audit is cumbersome and presents a more invasive process to the workday. Second, it is obviously more expensive in terms of the use of resources. Many principals do not have access to these types of collection devices. Third, it can be discouraging to principals who become overwhelmed if the audit produces extreme results that signal the need to make significant changes.

Why Consider a Time Audit?

Your first reaction might be to skip the notion of a time audit and move onto the next chapter. You can do this and still make significant gains in your leadership practices. A time audit won't necessarily contribute to the success of your plan to alter leadership practices. However, I would be remiss if I did not make a case for why you might want to consider this enhancement to your overall audit. Previous time studies of school leadership show that, on average, principals spend less than 20–30 percent of their workday in areas that contribute to improved teaching and learning (Berkey, 2008b; Archer, 2004). The advantage to conducting a time audit is that it allows the principal to get a handle on the balance of hours devoted to various areas of school management and leadership. It provides a baseline measurement and reference point for ongoing comparisons as principals shift the focus of their work. It also quantifies the use of time, which can be a concrete measure of improvement.

Some Options to Conduct Your Own Time Audit

If you decide to conduct a time audit of your leadership, the following options would be worthy of consideration in settings where you don't have substantial resources. Although not perfect, they can provide you with a quantitative analysis of your daily practices.

1. Use an Observer

Think about using a volunteer who would be willing to follow you around and record your activities. Find someone familiar with school leadership so that the training and preparation will be kept to a minimum. Retired school principals, university professors, or interns preparing for the principalship are good sources. To make it easier for the recorder, split your audit into half days with a goal of capturing the equivalent of two full days of data. Using more than one auditor has reliability issues, but if it gets the job done it is better to capture multiple samples rather than just one. Once you have identified your observer(s), meet and review the process by which the data will be collected and set the dates on your calendars. Figures 5.2 and 5.3 (following pages) display collection instruments that can be used to record time intervals throughout the process. Some studies record data as frequently as every five minutes, but for the purposes of your time audit every 15 minutes is adequate. Use the Leadership Audit to categorize how each 15-minute interval was used. Once the data has been collected, calculate the percentage of time associated with each of the 10+ categories and save your results for future time audits. This is your baseline.

2. Use Your Secretary

Another technique is to ask your secretary to record the times throughout the day when you are in and out of your office. Give your secretary the opportunity to quiz you as you leave and as you return on how you are spending your time. Again, use half-day audits to make it less stressful on yourself and your secretary. At the end of each audit, use the Leadership Audit instrument to categorize the time and data recorded, and calculate your results.

3. Use Yourself

This is perhaps the most difficult to accomplish, but for the strong willed and disciplined, it can work. Using a pad of paper, or for the technology proficient,

Figure 5.2. Time Audit (AM)	
Date: ___ / ___ / ___ Observer:_____	
AM	**Description of Activity**
6:30–6:45	
6:45–7:00	
7:00–7:15	
7:15–7:30	
7:30–7:45	
7:45–8:00	
8:00–8:15	
8:15–8:30	
8:30–8:45	
8:45–9:00	
9:00–9:15	
9:15–9:30	
9:30–9:45	
9:45–10:00	
10:00–10:15	
10:15–10:30	
10:30–10:45	
10:45–11:00	
11:00–11:15	
11:15–11:30	

\multicolumn{2}{c}{**Figure 5.3. Time Audit (PM)**}
\multicolumn{2}{l}{Date: ___/___/___ Observer:_____}
PM	**Description of Activity**
12:00–12:15	
12:15–12:30	
12:30–12:45	
12:45–1:00	
1:00–1:15	
1:15–1:30	
1:30–1:45	
1:45–2:00	
2:00–2:15	
2:15–2:30	
2:30–2:45	
2:45–3:00	
3:00–3:15	
3:15–3:30	
3:30–3:45	
3:45–4:00	
4:00–4:15	
4:15–4:30	
4:30–4:45	
4:45–5:00	

some type of PDA, make an entry for yourself each time you switch the focus of your work throughout the morning or afternoon. Again, half days will be much easier, and as in the previous two cases, think about four half-day collections.

Final Thoughts on the Audit

In this chapter we examined the purpose, content, and steps of conducting an audit of how you spend a typical workday. Qualitative and quantitative methods were reviewed as a means of collecting data that will provide you with rich information to be analyzed in the next chapter. While every attempt to simply the process has been made, it is equally important to understand that no process will succeed unless you have made a commitment to using it and following through. Now let's take a look at how to analyze the results.

Chapter 6
The Leadership Analysis

You cannot teach a man anything; you can only help him to discover it in himself.

—GALILEO GALILEI

It would be nearly impossible to make the case that school principals are not busy people. They hit the ground running and manage a mountain of tasks and responsibilities that don't let up until the kids and the adults leave campus at the end of the day. Yet, the key challenge facing school leaders is that of effectiveness. John Maxwell (1995) warned leaders that, "Activity is not necessarily accomplishment." Effective leaders know how to prioritize their work around purposeful activity that contributes to the attainment of the goals of the organization. In this chapter we will use the data collected during the Leadership Audit to analyze the impact of leadership activities on the capacity to improve teaching and learning.

Connecting Behaviors with Intended Outcomes

I have been blessed with an excellent personal physician. Every time I go in for my annual physical, he starts with a discussion of what I want to achieve with my wellness for the coming year. He asks me to describe in detail how I behave throughout each day and takes notes on eating and sleeping habits, exercise practices, work routines, and how I relax. He leads me through a thoughtful analysis of how each behavior relates to my wellness goals so that I have a clear understanding of what to continue, what to stop, and what to modify. I have also noticed that he never judges what I do. He simply offers what he knows from medical research and leaves the critiquing up to me. I have come to realize that the real expert on my behavior patterns is myself and that real change will only come from my personal analysis of those behaviors that need to be accelerated and those that need to be modified or extinguished.

The Leadership Analysis takes the same approach. It allows the principal to identify leadership behaviors that connect with the improvement of teaching and learning and the ones that simply do not. Not all of the practices will fall neatly on opposite ends of the spectrum. In fact, many will be somewhere in between. Some will be partially aligned with your goals while others will be further away. The purpose of the Leadership Analysis is to identify those leadership behaviors that should be targeted for more attention, those that need to be modified, as well as those that should be discontinued.

Leadership is Personal

In his book, *Leadership is an Art*, Max DePree (1989) made the case that leadership is learned over time and that, "Leaders can delegate efficiency, but they must deal personally with effectiveness." At the center of effectiveness is the leader's ability to present a high level of credibility to the organization. Leadership is very personal and the challenges that school leaders face more than ever is to not only talk about the improvement of teaching and learning, but to model a personal commitment to it through daily practices. Kouzes and Posner (1995) in their landmark book, *The Leadership Challenge*, revealed that when members of an organization perceive their leader to be credible, they are more likely to feel proud, possess a sense of team spirit, see their values as aligned to those of the organization, feel committed, and hold a sense of ownership.

The Changing Role of the Principal

Over the past two decades a higher level of importance has been placed on the instructional leadership role of the principal. Today's principal must possess specific knowledge of curriculum, instruction, and assessment along with the skills to effectively engage professionals in meaningful work that improves teaching and learning. The challenge for school principals is to ratchet up their instructional leadership while shrinking the traditional role expectations of their jobs. It then should be no surprise that when principals take a close look at their time investment in existing roles, much of it is consumed by work that does not link with improving the academic results of their students.

The Leadership Analysis Process

The Leadership Analysis involves a careful examination of the daily practices collected in the Leadership Audit in relationship to the capacity to improve teaching and learning. Using a rubric, the principal evaluates each item listed under the 10+ categories and records these on a Likert scale. As each general area is analyzed, two things begin to happen. First, a general understanding of the present condition of one's leadership emerges. Second, ideas and strategies for change begin to take shape.

The Leadership Rubric

The Leadership Rubric represents degrees of perception, and therefore it is important to understand that it is limited in terms of reliability. First, it relies on the user's level of understanding of those areas of leadership that have a strong influence on teaching and learning. Examples of how the rubric has been used by other principals will be provided, but I caution the reader to pause and consider an important reality. For those who are uncomfortable with their level of understanding of instructional leadership, it would be worth the time to read chapters 9–15 and other sources listed in the Appendices before proceeding with the Leadership Analysis process. Appropriate use of the rubric will depend on the user's understanding of instructional leadership skills.

Having disclosed this limitation, it has been my experience that principals have used the rubric effectively because it allows them to use the best experts on their present leadership practices, that being themselves. No one else can be a better judge of what was actually happening when the principal recorded entries in the auditing process. As you will see in the examples provided, placing the leadership practice back into the context in which it was performed allows the analysis to become a powerful force for self-reflection and change.

The rubric asks a simple, yet direct question:

To what degree does this practice influence the improvement of teaching and learning on your campus?

The response options on the rubric range from weak to strong in relationship to the improvement of learning:

Weak: Bears little or no relationship to the improvement of learning for every child. This item appears to be a traditional managerial task that does not require knowledge of curriculum, instruction, and assessment. Typically justified as an important responsibility, it is usually operational in nature and routine in delivery.

Mild: Has some relationship to the improvement of learning for every child. This item could be classified as supportive of structures and processes that build capacity in the school for improved learning. However, this item falls short of direct involvement in the instructional process and collaboration with teachers to improve student achievement.

Moderate: Has a relationship to the improvement of learning for every child. This item demonstrates a daily effort to support the instructional process through direct contact with students and teachers in the instructional setting. Performance of this item is grounded in collaborative work with teachers to improve curriculum, instruction, and assessment.

Strong: Has an influential relationship to the improvement of learning for every child. This item demonstrates out-of-the-box thinking to support the instructional process. This item requires a deep understanding of curriculum, instruction, and assessment and engages teachers in collaborative work to strengthen academic achievement.

Notice that the descriptors reference relationships to improved learning as well as the skill level necessary to perform the task or responsibility. As you will see in the following examples, the context in which the work is performed will influence the rating. This is why there will be a place on the instrument for the principal to make some notes for future reference.

A complete sample Leadership Analysis form (Figure 6.1) shows what we want to accomplish in this process. A blank version (Figure 6.2) follows on page 58.

Step 1: Gather all of the Leadership Audits and select one of the 10+ general areas for analysis.

Step 2: Rank each item using the rubric and checking the appropriate box.

Step 3. Write a short note that will help to explain the context of your rating. In other words, explain why you assigned the rating, based on how you performed the work.

Step 4. After completing all of the ratings, move onto the next area and repeat until all 10+ areas have been analyzed. Put your Leadership Analysis forms in a safe place. They will be used in the Leadership Transformation described in the next chapter.

Remember that there is no magic to the rating other than bringing one's work habits to a level of consciousness. It is also important to capture the rationale for your rating by making some brief notes. These will be useful in the next chapter when we develop strategies to improve leadership practices.

Figure 6.1. Leadership Analysis
Area of Responsibility: Parents and Community
Directions: List each item from the Leadership Audit. Check the descriptor that best identifies the item. Make notes that support your rating.
Weak: Bears little or no relationship to the improvement of learning for every child. This item appears to be a traditional managerial task that does not require knowledge of curriculum, instruction, and assessment. Typically justified as an important responsibility, it is usually operational in nature and routine in delivery.
Mild: Has some relationship to the improvement of learning for every child. This item could be classified as supportive of structures and processes that build capacity in the school for improved learning. However, this item falls short of direct involvement in the instructional process and collaboration with teachers to improve student achievement.
(Cont'd.)

Figure 6.1. Leadership Analysis *(Continued)*

Moderate: Has a relationship to the improvement of learning for every child. This item demonstrates a daily effort to support the instructional process through direct contact with students and teachers in the instructional setting. Performance of this item is grounded in collaborative work with teachers to improve curriculum, instruction, and assessment.

Strong: Has an influential relationship to the improvement of learning for every child. This item demonstrates out-of-the-box thinking to support the instructional process. This item requires a deep understanding of curriculum, instruction, and assessment and engages teachers in collaborative work to strengthen academic achievement.

Item	Notes	Weak 1	Mild 2	Mod. 3	Strong 4
1. Parent meeting	Met with parent who wants to complain about her daughter's grades		✓		
2. Attended PTA meeting	Discussed parent volunteer program to support reading program		✓		
3. Rotary meeting	Attended weekly luncheon	✓			
4. Fire chief	Met with chief to review procedures for fire drill	✓			
5. Parent meeting	Met with parents of new student with giftedness in math		✓		
6. Parent/teacher meeting	Collaborated with parents of gifted math student and teacher on accelerated program			✓	
7. Open house	Met with PTA committee to design training for effective parenting in technology and study skills		✓		
8. Parent meeting	Met with parent who is upset over the price increase of student lunches	✓			
9. Meeting with resident	Neighbor complained about students cutting through his yard	✓			
10. Meeting with Girl Scout leaders	Discussed use of building after school	✓			

Figure 6.2. Leadership Analysis

Area of Responsibility:

Directions: List each item from the Leadership Audit. Check the descriptor that best identifies the item. Make notes that support your rating.

Weak: Bears little or no relationship to the improvement of learning for every child. This item appears to be a traditional managerial task that does not require knowledge of curriculum, instruction, and assessment. Typically justified as an important responsibility, it is usually operational in nature and routine in delivery.

Mild: Has some relationship to the improvement of learning for every child. This item could be classified as supportive of structures and processes that build capacity in the school for improved learning. However, this item falls short of direct involvement in the instructional process and collaboration with teachers to improve student achievement.

Moderate: Has a relationship to the improvement of learning for every child. This item demonstrates a daily effort to support the instructional process through direct contact with students and teachers in the instructional setting. Performance of this item is grounded in collaborative work with teachers to improve curriculum, instruction, and assessment.

Strong: Has an influential relationship to the improvement of learning for every child. This item demonstrates out-of-the-box thinking to support the instructional process. This item requires a deep understanding of curriculum, instruction, and assessment and engages teachers in collaborative work to strengthen academic achievement.

Item	Notes	Weak 1	Mild 2	Mod. 3	Strong 4

Sample Ratings

To become more familiar with this instrument, let's take a look at some of the possible ratings of sample items from each of the 10+ areas of the Leadership Audit. For each sample there are two different responses based on the context of the work performed by each principal.

Safe and Orderly Environment

Principal A spends one lunch period a day supervising students. Principal B makes periodic visits to the cafeteria to check on supervision and to counsel students and arrange tutoring for those in need.

Principal A

		Weak	Mild	Mod.	Strong
Item	Notes	1	2	3	4
Lunch room supervision	Daily supervision of kids during lunch	✓			

Principal B

		Weak	Mild	Mod.	Strong
Item	Notes	1	2	3	4
Lunch room visit	Counseled students in academic risk during their lunch time and arranged tutoring		✓		

Principal A acknowledged that cafeteria duty is routine in nature and does not connect with improving teaching and learning. Principal B viewed this role as supportive of the teaching and learning process.

Fiscal Management

Principal A reviews the status of all budget accounts every Monday afternoon to make sure that expenditures are staying within the budget plan. Principal B meets with the media specialist to look for ways to save money by switching to electronic reference materials. This allows the media specialist to redirect budget money for additional computers in the center.

Principal A

		Weak	Mild	Mod.	Strong
Item	Notes	1	2	3	4
Budget review	Review of accounts and expenditures	✓			

Principal B

		Weak	Mild	Mod.	Strong
Item	Notes	1	2	3	4
Budget strategy meeting	Meeting with media specialist to reduce costs of reference materials and redirect money for additional computers		✓		

Communication

Principal A writes a monthly newsletter that shares important information about school events and accomplishments. Principal B writes a monthly column in the parent newsletter that focuses on tools and processes for parents to use in helping their children succeed in school.

Principal A

		Weak	Mild	Mod.	Strong
Item	Notes	1	2	3	4
Parent newsletter	Prepared monthly newsletter	✓			

Principal B

		Weak	Mild	Mod.	Strong
Item	Notes	1	2	3	4
Parent newsletter	Prepared column on parenting skills		✓		

Instructional Leadership

Principal A uses the district checklist to conduct a classroom observation. The principal meets with the teacher for a post-conference and offers positive feedback and a few suggestions for improvement. Principal B conducts walk-through observations with pairs of teachers as part of a training session to prepare them for peer observations and instructional coaching.

Principal A

		Weak	Mild	Mod.	Strong
Item	Notes	1	2	3	4
Teacher observation	Observation followed by post-conference with teacher			✓	

Principal B

Item	Notes	Weak 1	Mild 2	Mod. 3	Strong 4
Teacher walk-throughs with teachers	Walk-through with pair of teachers to train them in peer observation and instructional coaching				✓

Event Supervision and Attendance

Principal A attends the Friday night football game and helps with supervision. Principal B attends a National Honor Society meeting to discuss the possibility of having members provide tutoring to students who are struggling in math.

Principal A

Item	Notes	Weak 1	Mild 2	Mod. 3	Strong 4
Football game	Attended home football game	✓			

Principal B

Item	Notes	Weak 1	Mild 2	Mod. 3	Strong 4
N.H.S. meeting	Attended the National Honor Society meeting to discuss tutoring program			✓	

Special Education and 504s

Principal A attends the annual reviews of special education students. Teachers and specialists run the meeting. The principal listens and signs the plan. Principal B attends the annual review of a special education student and asks for a postponement of the adoption of the plan in order to conduct additional academic testing of the student. The principal identifies the need for more data on the student's reading skill sets.

Principal A

Item	Notes	Weak 1	Mild 2	Mod. 3	Strong 4
Annual review	Attended meeting and signed plan		✓		

Principal B

Item	Notes	Weak 1	Mild 2	Mod. 3	Strong 4
Annual review	Called for additional reading assessments				✓

Parents and Community

Principal A attends the monthly PTA meeting and answers questions from parents about the upcoming events of the school. Principal B attends the PTA meeting to discuss a parent volunteer program that would provide tutoring for children who are struggling with their reading skills.

Principal A

Item	Notes	Weak 1	Mild 2	Mod. 3	Strong 4
PTA meeting	Attended monthly meeting	✓			

Principal B

Item	Notes	Weak 1	Mild 2	Mod. 3	Strong 4
PTA meeting	Discussed parent volunteer reading program			✓	

Staff

Principal A meets with a teacher during her conference period to listen to her request to go on a trip with a spouse and use a personal day. Principal B meets with a teacher to design a new data reporting process that will get assessment results in the hands of the reading teachers much faster.

Principal A

Item	Notes	Weak 1	Mild 2	Mod. 3	Strong 4
Meeting with teacher	Request to use a personal day	✓			

Principal B

Item	Notes	Weak 1	Mild 2	Mod. 3	Strong 4
Meeting with teacher	Designed data reporting process				✓

Facilities and Services

Principal A performs a walk-through of the building to discuss issues with the custodian. Principal B meets with the custodian to talk about the redesign of a room that could be used by parent volunteers who will be tutoring children in reading.

Principal A

Item	Notes	Weak 1	Mild 2	Mod. 3	Strong 4
Meeting with custodian	Routine walk-through of the building	✓			

Principal B

Item	Notes	Weak 1	Mild 2	Mod. 3	Strong 4
Meeting with custodian	Meeting to discuss redesign of room for tutoring students		✓		

Administrivia

Principal A completes a report for central office on the number of suspensions issued for the month. Principal B completes a report for central office that shows data that demonstrates that a pilot program that de-tracks language arts has produced higher levels of achievement among students previously assigned to a low-level track. The report includes a recommendation to de-track all lower-level language arts classes. A faculty committee co-authors the report with the principal.

Principal A

Item	Notes	Weak 1	Mild 2	Mod. 3	Strong 4
Report	Monthly report on school suspensions	✓			

Principal B

		Weak	Mild	Mod.	Strong
Item	Notes	1	2	3	4
Report	Report on de-tracking language arts				✓

Things to Remember

The examples that have been provided demonstrate several points to consider when you conduct your analysis. First, because principals have inherited a large number of managerial tasks that are not associated with the improvement of teaching and learning, reality begins to set in when you check many items as weak or mild. Don't take this personally. It is a normal outcome for many principals. Second, it is equally important to understand that the context of each task and responsibility can define the level of effectiveness of the leader. The examples listed above linked a number of traditional responsibilities with Principal A. The examples connected to Principal B moved closer to the types of work that effective principals can deliver if they keep the goal of improved teaching and learning at the center of their daily work.

Next Steps

Take some quality time to move through the analysis process. It is revealing and humbling, yet critically important to the next step. In chapter 7, we will look at how to improve your effectiveness by developing strategies to move your daily work away from areas that have little impact on improving teaching and learning and toward those that do. This is the most exciting part of the process. Get ready to tip the scales in the other direction!

Chapter 7

The Leadership Transformation

All labor that uplifts humanity has dignity and importance and should be undertaken with painstaking excellence.

—MARTIN LUTHER KING, JR.

Not to be confused with transformational leadership, this chapter is about transforming the practices of the leader in ways that are congruent with the vision of the organization. Using the Leadership Analysis conducted in the previous chapter we will examine how principals can reshape their leadership around collaborative work that impacts curriculum, instruction, and assessment. To accomplish this, we will develop strategies to reduce daily time in managerial responsibilities in order to free up valuable time for instructional leadership and improvement of teaching and learning.

Lessons from the Field of Leadership

Jim Collins (2001) made the case that the organizational practice of "crediting the leader" or "blaming the leader" contributes to a myth that a leader must be some type of larger-than-life person who holds the answers to all of the problems of the organization. Many of us have been on the receiving end of this expectation and as Collins pointed out, it holds back the organization from doing great things. We have discussed at length the voluminous expectations placed on school principals. This chapter will provide tools that principals can use to alter daily work habits, distribute leadership, and become more effective. Before examining these processes an important question to consider is how to change the traditional roles of the principal within the context of an organization that holds onto an old paradigm. Experts in the field have offered several responses to this issue.

Walking the Talk

The call for schools to be held accountable for results has generated a discussion about the need for change to get improved outcomes. John Kotter (1996) pointed out that if leaders want to embrace change, they must communicate this through their behavior. Speeches, meetings, memos, and newsletters are all helpful in clarifying the vision, but if leaders don't model changes in their own daily practices, their credibility within the organization will wither. Kouzes and Posner (1995) drew the same conclusion in their 7th of *10 Commitments of Leadership*. Leaders, "set the example by behaving in ways that are consistent with shared values." It doesn't make sense to engage the faculty in discussions and work that is intended to ratchet up the quality of instruction in classrooms and then march off to daily cafeteria duty, or spend all of the after-school hours attending athletic events. If we are serious about leading improved learning, we must model this in our daily behaviors.

Learning to Say No

Effective leaders learn to say no to things that consume their energy and distract them from the work that improves results. Many times I have heard principals complain that they would like to devote more time to leading instruction, but other priorities get in the way. Stephen Covey (1989) reminded us that leadership is about choices and when we select what gets our attention, by default we say no to others. The volume of time to get things done is finite, and therefore the issue is how leaders choose to spend it. Covey acknowledged that emergencies arise, but when leaders spend more time planning, building relationships, and seizing opportunities, they experience fewer crises. For example, when community members want you to meet during school hours, just say no by suggesting an alternative time outside of the school day. Staying on campus and working with teachers to improve learning for all children will have a much higher payback in the form of improved student achievement and happier children who succeed.

Reframing the Problem

Phil Schlechty has been one among the talented and prolific writers on the topic of school change and leadership. In his book, *Shaking Up the School House* (2001), Schlechty revealed that leaders need to know how to reframe problems. He pointed out that often, leaders solve problems in the same manner in which they arrive at their doorstep. Eventually, the problem returns. Instead, he suggested that leaders define problems in new ways that are convincing to those they want to support the change. For example, many principals invest a considerable amount of time attending annual review meetings for special education students. Yet, in many cases, principals are not needed because the professionals have done their work to everyone's satisfaction. Some special education staff want the principal at all meetings in the event there is a hostile parent or a demanding advocate. Other districts require the principal to be there out of fear that special education staff will make costly promises in the form of staffing and resources. The question could be reframed around:

What would it take to make special education staff confident in and central office trusting of an annual review process that is conducted without the presence of the principal?

Investing in a minimum amount of planning could achieve a harmonious resolution that could be sustained over time. Reframing problems can be a useful skill in the transformation of the roles of the principal.

The Leadership Transformation Plan

The purpose of the Leadership Transformation Plan is to help principals develop strategies that, over time, will cause significant shifts in their daily leadership practices by reducing time in areas that are non-essential to effective leadership, and increasing time in those areas that are essential. Using the Leadership Analysis conducted in the previous chapter, you will make decisions about your existing practices in one or more of four ways:

1. Eliminate: This practice should be discontinued. It does not warrant the direct involvement of the principal.
2. Restructure: This practice should be modified to reduce the time investment of the principal.
3. Reassign: This practice should be shared with someone else in the organization.
4. Enhance: This practice should receive additional attention.

Before we discuss these decisions in further detail, it is important to note that there are no hard and fast rules for making them other than to allow the Leadership Analysis you conducted in the previous step to serve as your guide. Principals will have different perspectives on what will or will not work in their campus setting. Politics, culture, and varying degrees of autonomy each have an influence on the strategies that will work. The bottom line is that in order to change the emphasis of one's daily leadership, decisions will have to be made about what goes, what stays, and what gets altered.

Strategies to Eliminate

There are certain things that principals should not do. My personal method of examining this was to ask myself if the task or practice required the training I received to become a principal. If it didn't, I concluded that I probably should not spend a lot of time on it. This does not mean that I completely refrained from engaging in these activities. Sometimes principals have to perform tasks to send the message that there are things that all adults should share, such as visibility in hallways when students change classes. But problems arise when servant leadership is misinterpreted to mean that there is no task too small for the leader to be seen performing. I have witnessed principals justifying why they sweep halls, pick up in the cafeteria, distribute keys to the staff, and so forth. Public schools are in a crisis mode, and the time of the principal is so critical that it doesn't make sense to spend it on small tasks when student learning is at stake. Therefore, the elimination category is about letting go. Here are just a few samples of things that principals should consider eliminating from their work:

- Inventorying textbooks
- Ordering supplies
- Checking time sheets of classified staff
- Holding detentions
- Supervising athletic events

This list can go on, but you get the idea. Several of these are tasks that someone needs to take care of, but ones that most principals would agree do not require their direct involvement. Others are practices that principals can decide to discontinue altogether.

Strategies to Restructure

In many cases, principals find that they don't want to entirely step away from a practice, but would like to restructure the responsibility for a couple of reasons. First, thinking about the previous discussion of reframing a problem, there might be an opportunity to change the emphasis of the work so that it can be refocused on the vision of the campus. Second, by restructuring a given practice, the principal's involvement can be reduced in a way that not only saves time, but allows the principal to conduct work that more closely resembles instructional leadership. For example, many principals engage in building the master schedule for the coming school year. Anyone who has done this knows that there is a plethora of tasks involved. Recent advancements in scheduling software have eased some of this, but much of it continues to be intense administrivia. In many cases the master schedule is developed around the priority of making sure that all children get scheduled into where they need to be. This is a traditional view of scheduling, and therefore much of the work can be performed by someone other than the principal. However, we know that if schools are going to improve, a higher level of ongoing, collaborative work must take place. A principal could rephrase the question as follows:

What would it take to create a master schedule that embeds daily time for teachers to collaborate on important curriculum, instruction, and assessment issues that lead to improved student achievement?

In answering this question, the principal's role in the master schedule could shift from hands-on, detailed work, to discussions with teachers in the design of a highly collaborative work schedule that is focused on the vision of the school. Once the model is developed, the detailed work of the master schedule could be distributed among those in the organization who have a stake in the final product, such as teachers and counselors.

Here are some samples of responsibilities that are worthy of restructuring:

Traditional Role of the Principal	Restructured Role of the Principal
Evaluation of instruction via observations	Coaching of instruction via walk-throughs
Writing and directing school improvement plans and processes	Facilitating and supporting grade/subject- level learning teams to improve curriculum, assessment, and instruction
Attending the majority of athletic and extracurricular events	Creating a schedule that provides intermittent visibility at events
Writing the parent newsletter	Contributing an article to the parent newsletter
Handling student discipline and attendance referrals from staff	Providing teachers with effective classroom management skills and strategies
Planning and leading the monthly staff meeting	Attending team meetings and providing teachers with feedback on their teamwork

Strategies to Reassign

A good part of the daily work of principals can be reassigned to someone else in the organization, depending on the level of responsibility, the skills of the person who will perform the work, and the level of authority required. Reassignment not only frees up time for the principal, but equally important, it presents an opportunity to distribute leadership. Effective principals help others grow professionally through the reassignment of work that becomes challenging and rewarding for the individual. Notice that I have avoided the use of the word delegation. Sometimes people react to this term because it implies a top down management style. However, for purposes of understanding how to delegate, it makes sense to examine current thinking in this field.

The art of delegation has been studied and refined by experts in management. Three important elements (Lowe, 2008) are involved in delegating work to others:

- ♦ Responsibility
- ♦ Authority
- ♦ Accountability

Effective delegation occurs when both parties share an appropriate balance of each of these elements. When one delegates, you retain a portion of the responsibility for getting things done, provide the authority to see the task to completion, and share in the accountability for results. Before any delegation takes place, a two-way conversation needs to occur in which the supervisor clarifies what is to be delegated (reassigned) along with the degree of responsibility, authority, and accountability to be owned by each. The principal has a number of people who are highly capable of carrying forward many of the traditional roles associated with the position.

Principal's Secretary

It has been my experience that most secretaries not only want to be appreciated but respected as competent professionals. There can be no finer complement than to recognize this and give them greater responsibility and authority to complete important work and serve as an administrative assistant to the principal.

Sample items for reassignment:

- ♦ Budget implementation and oversight
- ♦ E-mail management
- ♦ Communication liaison for parent organizations
- ♦ Event planning

Assistant Principal

One of the greatest shortcomings of the role of the assistant principal is that the person gets trapped in a daily barrage of discipline and attendance issues. If principals are not attentive to this dilemma, there can be few opportunities for assistants to practice the skills that will prepare them to someday lead their own campuses.

Sample items for reassignment:

- ♦ The principal's designee at events and meetings
- ♦ Administrative liaison to grade level or department teams
- ♦ Staff development coordinator

Guidance Counselor

Guidance counselors are some of the most important people in helping a school remain focused on improved learning for every child. Through some basic reorganization of structures and processes, counselors can play a major role in instructional leadership by assisting the principal with important collaboration among the staff.

Sample items for reassignment:

♦ Oversight of data systems to inform teachers
♦ Coordination of services and processes to address learning problems
♦ Development and implementation of the master schedule
♦ Engagement of parents in the learning process of their children

Teacher Leaders and Teacher Teams

Teachers take greater ownership in the improvement of teaching and learning when they are empowered with responsibility and authority over those factors that will make their work effective and satisfying. This begins with a sincere commitment to enable teacher leaders and teams of teachers to become powerful participants in the school. Teachers should be involved in the budget; recruitment and selection of staff; and the improvement of curriculum, instruction, and assessment in ways that are collaborative and shared with the principal. Sample items for reassignment:

♦ Budget preparation
♦ Teacher recruitment and selection
♦ Instructional improvement
♦ Enhancement of curriculum and assessment

Support Staff

Support staff can take greater responsibility and authority for their work in ways that ratchet up their leadership and ability to contribute to the mission and vision of the school. Engaging the custodial, food service, security, and student support staff in a meaningful dialogue of how they can step into leadership roles that have a direct impact on the ability of the school to succeed is an important consideration for the principal.

Sample items for reassignment:

♦ Campus safety and security planning
♦ Food service evaluation and improvement
♦ Transportation troubleshooting
♦ Clerical support for teaching staff

Strategies to Enhance

As you conducted the Leadership Analysis, you will also identify habits and practices that contribute to the vision of the school, but don't get enough of your time. Not only are these items worthy of more attention, they can be refined, improved, and lifted to a higher level of effectiveness in your leadership practices. This is an opportunity to develop strategies that will drive your leadership deeper into those areas that count in the improvement of teaching and learning. Here are some examples.

Present Practice	Enhanced Practice
Review of report cards to identify students in need of academic assistance	Meetings each week with teams of teachers to identify students in need of academic assistance
Planning in-service days with a committee of teachers	Embedding staff development into the workday
Providing teachers with suggestions on how to improve instruction	Co-teaching with teachers to model strategies for improvement

Working Your Plan

The Leadership Transformation Plan is nothing more than a process to get you moving in the direction of higher levels of effectiveness by investing more of your valuable time in areas that count. By itself, the plan means nothing. With a sufficient amount of passion, vision, and courage, it can be your launch pad to doing what you have always wanted to do, but had no time. It also represents an attitude that if you are going to get others to change, you must model it through a day-to-day, deliberate effort to transform your own leadership:

Step 1: Select a general area from your Leadership Analysis
Step 2: Select a specific task or responsibility from the general area
Step 3: Decide to eliminate, restructure, reassign, or enhance the item
Step 4: Identify a strategy to implement the change

Figure 7.1 illustrates the Leadership Transformation Plan that will help you move through the four steps of transforming daily practices to improve the effectiveness of your work.

Listed below are sample items and strategies to get you thinking about your own plan. Notice that in some cases, you can combine eliminating and reassigning, depending on the specifics of your strategy. Again, not everyone will agree with every given approach. These must be customized with and aligned to the circumstances and conditions in each school setting.

A blank version of this form, Figure 7.2, can be found on page 74.

Figure 7.1. Leadership Transformation Plan

General Area of Responsibility _Administrivia_

Directions: List each item from your Leadership Analysis and determine if you will eliminate, restructure, reassign, or enhance this item in order to transform your leadership to one that is deeply rooted in daily work to improve teaching and learning.

Item #1 _Collecting and reviewing weekly lesson plans_

☑ Eliminate	☐ Restructure	☐ Reassign	☐ Enhance

Strategies: Announce at faculty meeting and clarify that lesson plans should always be available in the classroom in the event of an observation or walk-through.

Item #2 _Completing purchase orders_

☑ Eliminate	☐ Restructure	☑ Reassign	☐ Enhance

Strategies: Train secretary to complete purchase order forms—all items ready for signature.

Item #3 _Approval of periodic teacher requests for classroom supplies_

☐ Eliminate	☑ Restructure	☐ Reassign	☐ Enhance

Strategies: Order and distribute all classroom supplies at the beginning of the school year.

Item #4 _Collecting and distributing keys to teachers_

☐ Eliminate	☑ Restructure	☐ Reassign	☐ Enhance

Strategies: Allow teachers to keep their keys over the summer and only collect them in the event of a change in assignment, retirement, or resignation.

Item #5 _Arranging for substitute teachers for teachers with planned absences (non-emergency)_

☑ Eliminate	☑ Restructure	☑ Reassign	☐ Enhance

Strategies: Train secretary to coordinate the arrangement of substitutes for planned absences of teachers (personal, medical) for non-emergency stiuations.

Item #6 _Preparing and posting fire drill signs in classrooms_

☑ Eliminate	☐ Restructure	☑ Reassign	☐ Enhance

Strategies: Reassign to head custodian and have him sign off on a checklist of classrooms that all signs were posted.

Item #7 _Meeting with class ring and senior announcement company representatives_

☑ Eliminate	☐ Restructure	☐ Reassign	☑ Enhance

Strategies: Have representatives contact the class advisors directly and allow the advisors to determine if they want to meet with representatives

Figure 7.2. Leadership Transformation Plan

General Area of Responsibility _____

Directions: List each item from your Leadership Analysis and determine if you will eliminate, restructure, reassign, or enhance this item in order to transform your leadership to one that is deeply rooted in daily work to improve teaching and learning.

Item #1 _____

☐ Eliminate	☐ Restructure	☐ Reassign	☐ Enhance

Strategies:

Item #2 _____

☐ Eliminate	☐ Restructure	☐ Reassign	☐ Enhance

Strategies:

Item #3 _____

☐ Eliminate	☐ Restructure	☐ Reassign	☐ Enhance

Strategies:

Item #4

☐ Eliminate	☐ Restructure	☐ Reassign	☐ Enhance

Strategies:

Item #5 _____

☐ Eliminate	☐ Restructure	☐ Reassign	☐ Enhance

Strategies:

Item #6 _____

☐ Eliminate	☐ Restructure	☐ Reassign	☐ Enhance

Strategies:

Item #7 _____

☐ Eliminate	☐ Restructure	☐ Reassign	☐ Enhance

Strategies:

Putting It All Together

In this chapter we examined some of the practices identified by experts in the field of leadership that will be useful in changing the daily work of the principal. Using the Leadership Analysis from the previous chapter, we looked at ways to eliminate, restructure, reassign, or enhance existing leadership responsibilities. Using a Leadership Transformation Plan, we started the process of mapping out a variety of strategies to alter the ways we perform daily leadership. In the next chapter we will pull all of the processes used in the first half of this book into a framework that will be easy to follow, and most important, to get short-term results leading to long-term gains.

Chapter 8

The Implementation Plan

The way to get started is to quit talking and begin doing.

—Walt Disney

One of the most gratifying yet challenging aspects of any plan for change is getting started and realizing initial results. Finding time has been the central focus of the first half of this book, and is the number one issue for school principals in scaling up the effectiveness of their leadership. Using the processes reviewed in previous chapters, we will design a sensible and achievable plan during the first 30 days of your leadership transformation. This will involve establishing baseline measurements, setting short- and long-term goals, committing to change, and scheduling actions. Getting into a routine of shedding old habits and practices involves risk taking, and many people get caught up in the fear of failure. Procrastination can be a powerful force to overcome, and thus we will begin with a review of some of the tips that leading authors on this topic have offered. The remainder of the chapter will be devoted to the preparation of your implementation plan.

Procrastination

Just like other human beings who face a variety of challenges, principals use coping skills to see them through the day. Instead of tackling issues head on, they learn to navigate around them. The downside to this behavior is that it limits the influence of leadership, according to the authors (Patterson, Grenny, Maxfield, McMillan, & Switzer, 2008) of the bestseller, *Influencer: The Power to Change Anything*. Successful leaders formulate and apply strategies to problems that others learned to cope with rather than address. Other writers in the field of behavior management agree on several root causes of procrastinating action and offer alternative perspectives on dealing with it.

Fear of Failure

Dr. William J. Knaus (1998), a leading source on the development of strategies to overcome procrastination and author of *Break the Habit...Now*, revealed that we spend a lot of energy visualizing how things could go wrong and thus avoid what appear to be painful consequences. He suggested that if we redefine our work as a series of experiments, it becomes easier to deal with the reality of failures as learning experiences that guide us to solutions. As we develop short- and long-term goals it will be important to view each strategy to reduce time in nonproductive work as a trial-and-error effort process, rather than an all-or-nothing scenario. Educators sometimes place themselves in a box by thinking that every action must be successful when we know that in order to make progress we have to accept a certain number of failed attempts before we get it right.

Discomfort with Criticism

It took me a long time to understand that criticism is a healthy and important part of leadership. When people provide you with negative feedback, it is an opportunity to understand their perspective; sort out what is important and aligned with your vision and beliefs; and build stronger relationships. Neil Fiore (1989), author of *Overcoming Procrastination*, recommends that if we are uncomfortable with criticism, we must learn how to suspend it in the short term in order to take action and get results. Otherwise, we will continuously alter our behavior based on what others want us to do or not do. Many of us have worked under leadership that continuously changes direction in an attempt to keep people happy. It never works. In the end, the organization becomes rudderless and people lose faith in leadership that does not have the courage to keep things on course.

Lack of Urgency

Hyrum Smith (1994), creator of the *Franklin Day Planner*, has successfully helped millions of people overcome the issue of procrastination by focusing on the need to create urgency in what we do. His formula is simple, yet direct—set deadlines to get things done. It sounds easy, but as Franklin fans have discovered, it requires a commitment to setting priorities with deadlines that require immediate action. Smith encouraged people to start with unpleasant work early in the day and make our plans into a game so that we feel challenged and on a mission. He also stressed the importance of building in short-term rewards that serve as an incentive to completing the tasks at hand. As we develop our transformation plan, we will use parts of Smith's formula by setting short- and long-term goals with specific deadlines so that our daily work begins to feel more productive and rewarding.

Too Many Obligations

Principals take on many tasks and responsibilities whether they are wanted or unwanted. Over time, the school principal's office has become the depository of too many obligations that add up to a lot of unproductive work leaving the principal not only overwhelmed, but unfulfilled. Smith suggested grounding more of one's daily work in areas that closely align with those that make a difference. His 3rd law of successful management states that, "When your daily activities reflect your governing values, you experience inner peace." The inner peace for the principals can be found in the satisfaction of spending more time in daily work that improves teaching and learning throughout the school.

Planning the Work:
The First 30 Days

The first half of this book focused on processes and strategies to shrink the volume of time that principals devote to tasks and responsibilities that are unrelated to improving the academic results of students. Now we will turn to putting it all together by first getting things in place and then implementing a month-by-month transformation plan.

Getting Ready Calendar

During the first 30 days there are several processes to initiate so that short-term and long-term plans can be developed. The following is a recommended schedule that can be followed prior to the first month of implementation:

Week 1
+ Select and order a 360° assessment (chapter 4)
+ Schedule a meeting with the superintendent to discuss your plan (chapter 3)
+ Schedule a meeting with your secretary (chapter 3)

Week 2
+ Conduct faculty and staff meetings to discuss your intentions (chapter 3)
+ Conduct one morning and one afternoon Leadership Audit (chapter 5)

Week 3
+ Conduct one morning and one afternoon Leadership Audit (chapter 5)
+ Conduct a Quantitative Time Audit (chapter 5) *Optional/Recommended

Week 4
+ Conduct the Leadership Analysis and Leadership Transformation (chapters 6–7)
+ Conduct the 360° assessment (chapter 4)
+ Create your Leadership Transformation Notebook and first-month plan (chapter 8)

Leadership Transformation Notebook

I have found it useful to keep all of the related documents together in either a three-ring binder or an electronic file. If done appropriately, this resource can become a professional development plan and meet many, if not all, of the district and state requirements for a principal's licensure renewal. The notebook can be used as a stand-alone daily planner, but also as an interface with a preferred daily planner system already in use.

TAB 1   360° Assessment Results

TAB 2   Leadership Audit

TAB 3   Quantitative Time Audit (optional/recommended)

TAB 4   Leadership Analysis

TAB 5   Leadership Transformation

TAB 6   Leadership Transformation Plan
  ◆ Monthly Transformation Plan/Time Reductions
  ◆ Monthly Plan to Increase Effectiveness
  ◆ Annual Plan to Increase Effectiveness

TAB 7   Principal Leadership Tracker

Working the Plan

The Monthly Plan

Every month you will work on strategies to accomplish two things. First, decrease time on managerial tasks and responsibilities, and second, increase time in instructional leadership.

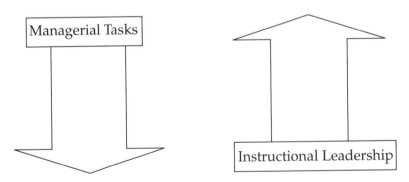

To facilitate monthly planning we will use two documents: one that is focused on reduction of time, and a second, focused on where to spend new captured time. In both cases, we will set monthly as well as annual goals, along with accompanying action plans. For now, we will review the time reduction side of the transformation plan and address the remainder in the second half of the book, after we have examined leadership work that influences improved academic achievement.

Goal Setting at Work

In chapter 4 we reviewed the SMART goal-setting process as a tool to ensure that we get results from our actions. Let's be clear on this part of the transformation plan. Our goal is to reduce daily time invested in work that is not directly related to those leadership areas that improve teaching and learning. Therefore, in both the short term and long term, goal attainment for this part of the plan should result in new time available for reallocation.

Setting goals for time reduction should begin with the work that came from the Leadership Analysis and Leadership Transformation strategies developed in chapters 6 and 7. Figure 8.1 (see page 82) displays the planning form we will use to develop monthly plans for the reduction of daily time in non-essential practices.

Start Small, Get Results

Experts in goal setting point out that too often, people set large goals that are only attainable over a long period of time, requiring multiple steps. The problem is that long-term goals are more difficult to sustain. For this reason, we will use a process that provides short-term goal setting and acquisition, along with monthly work on goals that are long term in nature. The purpose of this process is to get into a monthly rhythm of a focused effort to reduce time in non-essential areas so that we can redeploy valuable leadership time into those areas that will produce improved teaching and learning.

Two Shorts, One Long

The time reduction process follows the rationale that some of the strategies and processes to reduce daily time will take longer than others. There is no magic to determining the length of the goal or the time to successfully implement it. This must be balanced between the urgency for change and the unique factors associated with the workplace, including availability of resources and level of support. Use the process in ways that work for your campus. I have found it helpful to set two short-term goals that can be achieved within a month, plus one longer-term goal that will need to be achieved over several months.

Short-Term Goals

Setting goals that are achievable within a 30-day period allows the principal to focus on a few issues at a time and acquire some immediate results. Notice

Figure 8.1. Transformation Plan/Time Reduction Goals

TRANSFORMATION PLAN/TIME REDUCTIONS

Month: _____

General Area: _____   Item: _____

Short-Term Goal #1

SMART GOAL:
S ☐ _____
M ☐
A ☐ _____
R ☐
T ☐

Action Steps:

Week 1 _____
Week 2 _____
Week 3 _____
Week 4 _____

General Area: _____   Item: _____

Short-Term Goal #2

SMART GOAL:
S ☐ _____
M ☐
A ☐ _____
R ☐
T ☐

Action Steps:

Week 1 _____
Week 2 _____
Week 3 _____
Week 4 _____

General Area: _____   Item: _____

Long-Term Goal #____

SMART GOAL:
S ☐ _____
M ☐
A ☐ _____
R ☐
T ☐

Action Steps: Due Date

1st Month _____
2nd Month _____
3rd Month _____
4th Month _____
5th Month _____

that each goal has a SMART box to be checked as the goal is written. It is important to keep each goal in this format to ensure success. Some goals will require more collaborative time than others. For example, in Figure 8.2 (see page 84), the principal targeted the time devoted to reading and responding to e-mails during student contact time as an achievable short-term goal. The action steps to meet the goal involved collaboration with the secretary since most of this activity is limited to the personal work habits of the principal, whereas, the second short-term goal of reducing the hours spent on attending athletic events had an impact on a larger audience. If the principal attended fewer events, it could be viewed as diminishing support for athletics. Thus, one of the action steps involved collaborating with the coaching staff on the purpose and intent of the plan. In this situation, the principal found it valuable to talk to the coaches about being visible at home events, but not in attendance at all of them or for the full duration. Then, working with the secretary, the principal devised a plan to be visible at multiple home events scheduled for the same evening, therefore becoming more efficient with time and reducing the volume of hours consumed.

In Figure 8.3 (see page 85) we see an example of a change in procedure that will save time during student contact hours. This principal used part of a faculty meeting to discuss the need to shift meetings regarding personal issues to before and after school times. Because this could be viewed as inconvenient to faculty who are accustomed to seeing the principal on their lunch or conference time, it was important for the principal to engage the entire faculty in an open discussion and a rationale for the change. The principal also encouraged input from the faculty by using teachers considered to be part of the guiding coalition on campus as advisors in the development of the new process. Once a sensible plan was established, the principal also collaborated with the secretary to discuss process issues such as setting up appointments for teachers who need to discuss personal issues.

Notice that the short-term goals involve several action steps broken into weekly items that are not overwhelming to the principal, yet are specific to processes that move the goal to attainment. Again, the steps and process will be situational to the school campus and you will want to customize them accordingly. Do whatever it takes given your situation.

Long-Term Goals

There is no question that many of the changes you target will require multiple steps and collaborative processes that take more time. It is important to remind yourself that as you transform leadership practices, engage those affected by seeking input and using it to customize the steps towards goal attainment. For example, Figure 8.2 (see page 84) displays a plan that addresses a long-term goal of reducing the principal's daily time in discipline and atten-

Figure 8.2. Transformation Plan/Time Reductions: October

TRANSFORMATION PLAN/TIME REDUCTIONS

Month: October

General Area: Communication   **Item:**   E-mails

Short-Term Goal #1

SMART GOAL:

S	☑	Reduce the daily minutes spent reading and responding to e-mails
M	☑	
A	☑	during student contact time to zero within 30 days
R	☑	
T	☑	

Action Steps:

Week 1	Meet with secretary to discuss strategies and plans to reduce time.
Week 2	Give secretary access to my Outlook to practice sorting/deleting.
Week 3	Practice new system with secretary and troubleshoot issues.
Week 4	Practice reading and responding before/after student contact time.

General Area: Event Supervision and Attendance   **Item:**   Attending athletic events

Short-Term Goal #2

SMART GOAL:

S	☑	Reduce the hours spent attending athletic evens by 50% within the
M	☑	
A	☑	next 30 days.
R	☑	
T	☑	

Action Steps:

Week 1	Obtain copies of athletic calendars and develop a plan to be visible.
Week 2	Meet with coaches and athletic director to review plan and purpose.
Week 3	Set up a schedule that facilitates efficient use of time and visits.
Week 4	Implement new plan.

General Area: Safe and Orderly Environment   **Item:**   Attendance and Discipline Issues

Long-Term Goal #1

SMART GOAL:

S	☑	Reduce the daily time spent on direct involvement in student
M	☑	
A	☑	attendance and disciplinary issues by 50% within five months.
R	☑	
T	☑	

Action Steps:		**Due Date**
1st Month	Address the issue of ownership in the next faculty meeting.	Oct. 31
2nd Month	Establish a faculty committee to collaborate on new processes.	Nov. 30
3rd Month	Faculty committee collaborates with faculty on proposals.	Dec. 31
4th Month	Recommendations of committee discussed and finalized by faculty.	Jan. 31
5th Month	Implementation of new processes and procedures.	Feb. 28

Figure 8.3. Transformation Plan/Time Reductions: November

TRANSFORMATION PLAN/TIME REDUCTIONS

Month: November

General Area: Staff   **Item:** Meetings with teachers (personal)

Short-Term Goal #1

SMART GOAL:

S	☑	Reduce the daily minutes devoted to meetings with teachers regarding
M	☑	
A	☑	personal issues, during student contact hours, to zero within 30 days
R	☑	
T	☑	

Action Steps:

Week 1   Review this issue at the next faculty meeting and seek input.
Week 2   Collaborate with guiding coalition (faculty) on new progress.
Week 3   Finalize process using feedback from guiding coalition.
Week 4   Review process with secretary (appointment book) and implement.

General Area: Fiscal Management   **Item:** Purchase Orders

Short-Term Goal #2

SMART GOAL:

S	☑	Reduce the daily minutes devoted to processing purchase orders
M	☑	
A	☑	during student contact hours, to zero.
R	☑	
T	☑	

Action Steps:

Week 1   Meet with secretary and discuss strategies, processes and plans.
Week 2   Share new process with faculty and staff.
Week 3   Practice new process (sign-offs at end of work day).
Week 4   Meet with secretary and get feedback and make adjustments.

General Area: Safe and Orderly Environment   **Item:** Cafeteria Supervision

Long-Term Goal #2

SMART GOAL:

S	☑	Reduce the daily time spent supervising students in the cafeteria
M	☑	
A	☑	from 40 minutes to intermittent visits, within the next four months.
R	☑	
T	☑	

Action Steps:		Due Date
1st Month	Review issue with assistant principal and discuss options.	Nov. 30
2nd Month	Examine faculty and staff assignments for second semester	Dec. 31
3rd Month	Meet with underutilized staff member and train for second semester.	Jan. 31
4th Month	Implement new plan and check in on staff member.	Feb. 28

dance issues. Again, this is situational and some principals might not spend any daily time in this area if they have assistants or others in charge of these responsibilities. But in many cases, principals are involved because they find themselves in school cultures where the level of ownership by teachers and staff is limited. In this situation, the principal set a goal of reducing daily time in these areas by 50 percent and allocated a period of five months to achieve the goal. The action steps appropriately involved the faculty in a big picture discussion of the issues and an invitation to participate in a collaborative process to embed ownership among all adults through shared responsibility. Notice that the plan provided monthly action steps that engaged a variety of adults in the decision-making process, culminating in new approaches to be implemented in the fifth month. Each of the action steps had due dates at the end of each month. This ensured that the plan took shape and goal attainment was eventually reached.

In another example located in Figure 8.3 (see page 85), the principal inherited a campus practice whereby the preceding principal shared this responsibility with the assistant principal, each supervising one of the two lunch periods. The action steps engaged a variety of people in the collaboration of an alternative plan, starting with the assistant principal, and in turn, those adults who were underutilized for the coming semester. Experienced principals know that there are certain adults who don't have full schedules of responsibilities and thus are assigned to a variety of tasks to fill part of their workday. In this situation, the principal made the decision to use one or more individuals to cover lunch supervision. In some cases this could be paraprofessional staff while in others, instructional staff. It goes without saying that it would be preferable to use staff other than teachers first, before resorting to the use of underutilized teaching staff. Notice that the assigned number of the long-term goal is sequential from month to month, since they spread over multiple months. It is important to transfer each action step of the long-term goals to the calendar/planner system that you utilize.

Practice, Practice, Practice

New practices need time to become embedded habits. This will only happen by making a daily effort to consciously practice the short-term goals over and over. Some people like to keep their short-term goals in view, such as on the refrigerator, desktop, computer screen, or in a daily planner. The idea is to start each day with some reflection time on what you want to practice and achieve. Long-term goals require attention as well, but not on a daily basis. These can be reviewed at the beginning and ending of each week in order to plan and advance each action step throughout the month. More importantly, by reviewing the goals and plans on a regular basis, short-term goal attainment will not only be achieved, but will provide motivation for you to keep going.

The Other Half of the Equation

As new time is freed up, it is imperative that you are ready to apply it to the practices that will move your transformation to higher levels of effectiveness. In the second half of the book, we will examine in detail the leadership practices and habits that have been identified in the research as influential in improving student achievement. We will end the book by using the SMART goal process to set short-term and long-term goals to reinvest the daily time of the principal in critical areas that improve teaching and learning.

Spending Time on What Really Counts

The second part of this book is devoted to effective leadership practices that aspiring and practicing school principals can use to improve teaching and learning in schools. Chapters 10–14 provide a close examination of each major area of the Effective Principal Tracker, a conceptual model that is grounded in numerous studies of the impact of school leadership on student achievement. Each area of the Tracker is broken down into specific leadership behaviors that, collectively, will improve the effectiveness of the school principal. Chapters 9 and 15 present a process to assist principals in practicing and sustaining these behaviors through establishing plans, setting personal goals, measuring progress, and reflecting on results.

The purpose of the Effective Principal Tracker is to provide school leaders with a means of aiming their daily work at targets that will bring about results. While there have been considerable studies of school leadership and numerous models to improve the performance of school principals, a simplified roadmap to help them has been elusive. Part of this is due to the complexity of bringing together overlapping competencies identified in studies conducted by leading institutions throughout the country. In addition, many of the emerging programs to assist principals employ the use of a model in conjunction with the deployment of expensive resources such as job coaches, specialized training and the use of personnel to assume the managerial responsibilities of the principalship. Most principals don't have access to these programs and resources. The Tracker allows principals to utilize existing resources in shifting daily practices into those areas of leadership behavior that are the focus of a national movement to improve school leadership.

It is also important for the readers to continue their own investigation of successful practices. Appendix C provides a list of references that served as the foundation for the development of the Tracker. New and enhanced studies of effective school leadership will continue to appear on the horizon, and utilizing the findings of these in practical applications will be the challenge for school principals. The Tracker not only provides a framework for action, but also a depository for new methods to be included in the daily repertoire of effective leadership practices.

Finally, tracking improved leadership does not have to be an overwhelming endeavor. The purpose of the Tracker is to provide a sensible approach to shifting daily behaviors in a manner that is balanced, gradual, and sustainable. There are no quick fixes to school leadership. The essential ingredient is the commitment of the individual to changing behaviors by sticking to a plan.

Chapter 9

The Effective Principal Tracker

Nothing is particularly hard if you divide it into small jobs.

—HENRY FORD

Being effective requires a sustained effort to align daily habits and practices with those that bring about desired results. In this chapter we will introduce the framework of the Effective Principal Tracker and provide ways to integrate best practices into the daily repertoire of the school principal. Contrary to what some may think, the working hours of school leadership are a finite quantity. Making the best of that time will be the focus of our attention as we reflect on two important questions:

1. Where should I invest my time in order to be more effective?
2. How can I align my daily habits with those areas?

Where to Invest Your Time

School leaders know that the largest portion of a campus budget is in the cost of salaries and benefits. Teachers by far, represent a school's greatest financial investment. Yet, how much time do leaders spend in tending to that investment? Teachers will tell you that they can count the number of times the principal has been in their classroom. For many, interaction with the principal is limited to faculty meetings, formal observations, and occasional committee work. If principals are to become more effective, they must shift a considerable amount of their time to those who have the greatest influence over student achievement, the faculty.

The Real Work of Schools

The real work of schools is learning. Roland Barth (1990) insisted that, "School is a place where students discover, and adults rediscover, the joys, the difficulties, and the satisfactions of learning." Few would contest his viewpoint.

89

But if we were to follow principals around for a day, we would conclude that the work of the classroom and the work of the principal rarely intersect. Couple this with a long-standing tradition of teachers working in isolation of one another, and it becomes clear that the learning of adults is somewhat limited on many school campuses. In recent years, schools have engaged in the implementation of professional learning communities to bring people together to share their learning and practice. However, Fullan (2008) warned us that, "They give the educators a false sense of progress, while the deeper cultural changes required for school improvement are not being tackled." He suggested that, "Rather, learning is developing the organization, day after day, within the culture."

Daily Interactions

Fullan is right. Improving a school requires the involvement of teachers and administrators in a collaborative culture that is tightly wrapped around the work of curriculum, instruction, and assessment. The complexity of these variables can only be effectively addressed by learning that is deeply rooted in daily interactions among the adults. These interactions will require the development of strong relationships between the principal and the staff. It requires a shift in culture whereby the principal is a regular visitor to classrooms, and meetings among teachers are held to engage in thoughtful discussion, analysis of data, problem solving, coaching, and team building. The culture must evolve so that everyone takes on the roles of teacher as well as learner, and relationships become interdependent.

Discovering the Sum of the Parts

Back when I was in college, I earned money during the summer months by working in a pallet factory. My job changed weekly as I took the place of some-one who was on vacation. I did everything from cutting lumber, to nailing and assembling pallets. I quickly learned something that would be valuable to me years later. First, by spending time in every work station, I was able to see how each part of the process fit together. This enabled me to witness how critical my measurement and cutting of the parts were to the assembly process. It provided me with a clear understanding of the power of knowing how interdependent the work of adults should be. Second, I also was able to work with almost everyone in the plant, and this allowed me to see how each personality contributed to the culture of the workplace. More than once I was able to mend fences between people, because I knew them better than they knew each other.

Organizations are made up of people and processes, and therefore it is essential for leaders to discover how all of these fit together, by getting into their work spaces and interacting with all of the players. This will only happen when the principal spends time discovering the work being done, and the personalities involved.

Leading with Purpose

Allow purpose to drive your daily work. If we operate on the premise that the work of the principal is to engage with other adults to learn and improve the school, then the focus begins to shift away from managerial tasks to those practices that have purpose. When teachers see principals in classrooms on a frequent basis, it sends the signal that the principal's work has greater purpose than the traditional duties that consume their time. Leading with purpose brings clarity to the mission and vision of the school culture.

Understanding the Tracker

The Effective Principal Tracker provides a framework that helps school principals change their daily work habits, and at the same time shift the culture toward expectations and processes that improve teaching and learning. It allows principals to move the culture in step with the changes being modeled in their leadership.

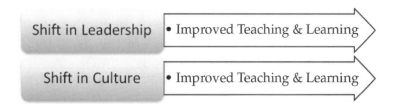

This approach has several advantages. First, it provides principals with a means of modeling the behaviors associated with a culture that is focused on improving teaching and learning. Second, it promotes shared learning and practice between principals and the other members of the school organization. It creates a comfort zone whereby people can experience the change process together. Third, it strengthens a common commitment to the important work of the classroom, and builds an enhanced respect for the daily challenges that teachers face.

The Five Components of the Tracker

Each of the five components of the Tracker represents an area of leadership practice that impacts student achievement through the engagement of principals and teachers in work to improve teaching and learning. All are well grounded in research and represent best practices for principals who want to lead effectively. There is no sequence to the components. Each can be applied at various times, to varying degrees. The model also suggests a balance of activity in each of the areas. It provides focus, yet flexibility in application.

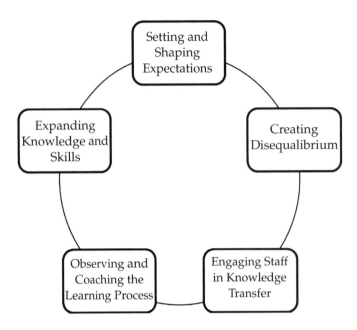

All of the five components have specific subcomponents that contribute to the effective leadership of the principal (Figure 9.1). Some of these will take priority over others during the implementation stage of the model. Others will be addressed as priorities shift and the effectiveness of the principal begins to climb. It is also important to remember that although the Tracker is a leadership framework, it is implemented through heavy engagement with teachers, students, staff, and members of the school community.

In most cases, there are subcomponents that should be addressed early on. Figure 9.2 (see page 94) illustrates those areas that are recommended as priorities when first implementing the Tracker. Each of these will be discussed at length in the following chapters.

Each subcomponent represents an opportunity for the principal to explore as daily time is freed up using the processes described in the first half of this book:

♦ Rebuilding passion by engaging people in discussions of the need for change sets an expectation for growth and improvement;
♦ Modeling change by spending less time in the office sends an immediate signal to staff that the principal is committed;
♦ Transferring best practices to help teachers inform their daily practices establishes the foundation for a culture that values the transfer of knowledge and information to improve performance;
♦ Walking through classrooms to observe and coach teachers begins to alter the perception from one that views the presence of the principal as evaluative to one that is supportive;
♦ Sharing experiences with other principals enables the leader to seek advice and build knowledge of best practices.

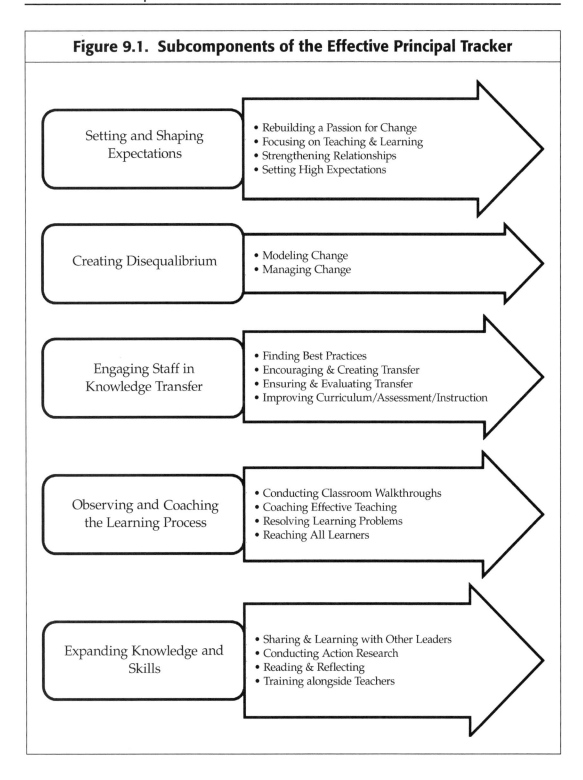

Figure 9.1. Subcomponents of the Effective Principal Tracker

Setting and Shaping Expectations
- Rebuilding a Passion for Change
- Focusing on Teaching & Learning
- Strengthening Relationships
- Setting High Expectations

Creating Disequalibrium
- Modeling Change
- Managing Change

Engaging Staff in Knowledge Transfer
- Finding Best Practices
- Encouraging & Creating Transfer
- Ensuring & Evaluating Transfer
- Improving Curriculum/Assessment/Instruction

Observing and Coaching the Learning Process
- Conducting Classroom Walkthroughs
- Coaching Effective Teaching
- Resolving Learning Problems
- Reaching All Learners

Expanding Knowledge and Skills
- Sharing & Learning with Other Leaders
- Conducting Action Research
- Reading & Reflecting
- Training alongside Teachers

As we will see in future chapters, the subcomponents of the Tracker provide a guide to practices that will scale up one's effectiveness in daily work that not only brings greater satisfaction to the principalship, but more important, produces better results for teachers and students.

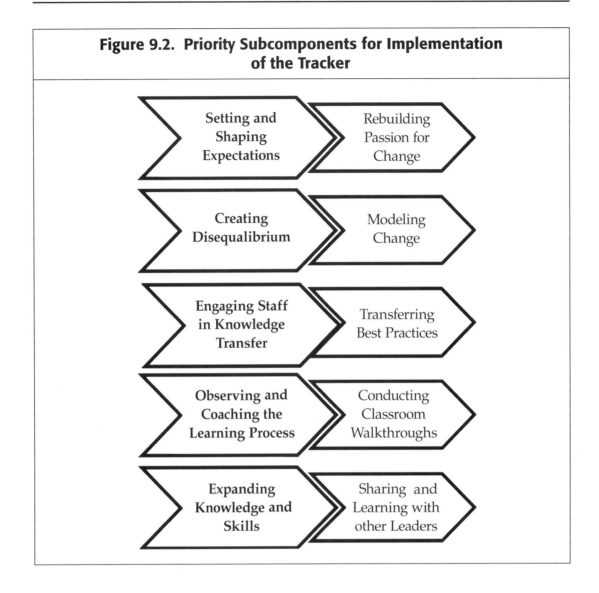

Figure 9.2. Priority Subcomponents for Implementation of the Tracker

How to Use the Tracker: Changing Habits

Using the Tracker is an easy and natural process because it incorporates short-term and long-term goals that can be integrated into any daily planner system. It begins with the establishment of annual goals that are broken down into monthly goals, weekly plans, and scheduled activity on one's daily calendar. Keeping in mind that this process is used parallel to efforts to reduce time in areas that do not contribute to effective leadership, it is important to go slow. Limit the number of goals that you set for yourself, especially in the beginning. You can always add more as you begin to experience the benefits of shifting your daily work into areas that bring results.

Annual Goals ⇨ Monthly Goals ⇨ Weekly Plans ⇨ Daily Planner

Annual Goals

When selecting annual goals it is important to take into consideration the overall picture of what you want to achieve during the school year. There should be a considerable amount of reflection that goes into your decision, and several inputs will be valuable in writing your goals. First, consider advice from those around you. The 360° feedback you conducted is a good place to identify areas for improvement in your leadership. You should also think about discussions you had with central office on the role of the principal and associated job description. Second, focus on the present culture of the school and think about goals that would allow you to not only change your leadership but move the school forward. Finally, remember to examine the priority list of subcomponents listed in Figure 9.2. Creating a need for change is a common issue on many school campuses. Then, take a copy of the Tracker (Figure 9.3) and begin to write a draft copy of one goal for each area of the Tracker. When writing the goals, use the SMART format and take into consideration the subcomponents of each part of the Tracker. For example, let's say you recognize from the 360° and discussions with central office that people are not clear on your expectations for the school. Your own perception tells you that teachers are satisfied with student results and see no need to change or improve. Thus, when writing an

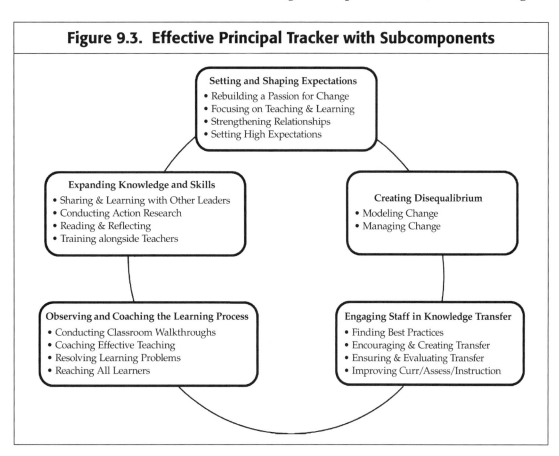

Figure 9.3. Effective Principal Tracker with Subcomponents

Setting and Shaping Expectations
- Rebuilding a Passion for Change
- Focusing on Teaching & Learning
- Strengthening Relationships
- Setting High Expectations

Expanding Knowledge and Skills
- Sharing & Learning with Other Leaders
- Conducting Action Research
- Reading & Reflecting
- Training alongside Teachers

Creating Disequalibrium
- Modeling Change
- Managing Change

Observing and Coaching the Learning Process
- Conducting Classroom Walkthroughs
- Coaching Effective Teaching
- Resolving Learning Problems
- Reaching All Learners

Engaging Staff in Knowledge Transfer
- Finding Best Practices
- Encouraging & Creating Transfer
- Ensuring & Evaluating Transfer
- Improving Curr/Assess/Instruction

annual goal for the Setting and Shaping Expectations component you examine the four subcomponents of the model and write the following goal:

<table>
<tr>
<td>

Setting and Shaping Expectations
Rebuilding Passion for Change
Focusing on Teaching and Learning
Strengthening Relationships
Setting High Expectations

</td>
<td></td>
<td>

Annual Goal: I will deepen a passion for change in the culture of the school and engage the faculty in the refinement of a vision by collaborating with them in the development of specific standards for curriculum, assessment, and instruction that are expected in every classroom

</td>
</tr>
</table>

Goals are not easy to write and will take multiple drafts until you are satisfied. It is also helpful to have someone else read them and provide you with feedback. Once you are satisfied with the goal, place it into the Annual Plan shown in Figure 9.4. The Annual Plan allows you to set a minimum of five goals for the year, with one coming from each of the five components of the Tracker. As we move through each of the components in the following chapters, there will be more examples of goals to study. For now, we will continue with the remaining steps in using the Tracker so that you get an understanding of the entire process.

Monthly Goals

The next step is to break each of the annual goals you have established into monthly goals. This is important for a couple of reasons. First, it allows you to set short-term, achievable goals that move you to long-term results. Second, it provides a focus of your leadership practices for the current month. When writing monthly goals it is important to think about the strategies that will achieve the annual goal as well as the sequence in which they must occur. Using the previous example, let's analyze the annual goal and identify strategies that

<table>
<tr>
<td>

Annual Goal: I will deepen a need for change in the culture of the school and engage the faculty in the refinement of a vision by collaborating with them in the development of specific standards for curriculum, assessment, and instruction that are expected in every classroom

</td>
<td></td>
<td>

♦ Need for change presentation
♦ Discussions with faculty
♦ Monthly reminders of need for change
♦ Review of vision statement
♦ Build need to revise vision
♦ New vision connected to classroom
♦ Curriculum, assessment, and instruction
♦ Collaborate on standards for the classroom
♦ Share new standards and discuss
♦ Identify next steps

</td>
</tr>
</table>

could be written into the form of monthly goals that are sequenced and achievable given the timeframe. It is helpful to first write some ideas next to the annual goal and then draft some month-to-month goals that accomplish each strategy.

Using the Annual Planner, write the monthly goals in the appropriate sequence. While it is possible to have more than one monthly goal for each of the annual goals, I suggest that you keep it simple in the beginning. Figure 9.4 shows a blank Annual Planner and Figure 9.5 on the following page a completed Annual Planner with the monthly goals inserted. Notice that each goal connects with the next and that some of them overlap, depending on the time estimated for completion. There is no hard and fast rule for setting monthly goals. The key is to take on what is realistic without going so slow that progress is not realized by yourself as well as the culture. Keep things moving.

Once you have filled in all of the monthly goals for an annual goal, copy them into the Monthly Planner shown in Figure 9.6 for the month. Using the August goal from our example, let's think of the action steps that will need to take place:

August Goal: I will deepen my own understanding of the need to change by studying internal and external factors that impact the future of education and the lives of our students.		**Actions:** ♦ Study the internal data that should cause our school to change and improve ♦ Study the external factors that should cause our school to change and improve ♦ Prepare an outline of findings to present ♦ Pepare a PowerPoint presentation on the need for change

Once the actions are determined, make an estimate of the time that will be required to complete each one and write it in the corresponding column. At this point you would continue to work through each of the monthly goals and place your actions for each on the monthly planner. The next step brings your goal planning to a level of reality by scheduling actions.

Weekly Planners

Hopefully you use some type of weekly planner for appointments and perhaps the scheduling of work. Regardless of the system you use, it is this point in the process that you will begin to schedule the specific actions into your calendar based on the time requirements you identified. Because these actions must be integrated with your other appointments, I recommend scheduling them no more than a month at a time. While actions to attain monthly and annual goals will be a priority, you also need to wrestle with changes you are making to reduce time in traditional areas of responsibility, so expect adjustments as you go along. As you schedule them, place a check in the last column of the

Figure 9.4. Effective Principal Tracker—Annual Plan with Monthly Goals

Subcomponent _____

Annual Goal:

Month	Monthly Goal
August	
September	
October	
November	
December	
January	
February	
March	
April	
May	
June	
July	

Figure 9.5. Effective Principal Tracker—Annual Plan with Monthly Goals

Setting and Shaping Expectations
Subcomponent

Annual Goal: I will deepen a need for change in the culture of the school and engage the faculty in the refinement of a vision by collaborating with them in the development of specific standards for curriculum, assessment, and instruction that are expected in every classroom.

Month	Monthly Goal
August	I will deepen my own understanding of the need to change by studying internal and external factors that impact the future of education and the lives of our students.
September	I will deepen the need for change in our school culture by engaging stakeholders in presentations and dialogue in the internal and external factors that impact the future of education and the lives of our students.
October	I will engage the faculty in a review of the vision statement of the school and get consensus on the need to revise the statement to reflect internal and external factors that impact the future of education and lives of our students.
November	I will engage the faculty in a collaborative process to revise the vision statement around the expectations of what needs to happen in every classroom on a daily basis in order to successfully prepare our students for the future.
December	I will work with the faculty to identify the standards we need for curriculum by examining what other countries are doing, what our universities and employers expect from students, and what experts in our field are recommending.
January	I will work with the faculty to prepare a draft of new standards for curriculum that will serve as a framework for the teachers and leaders to follow when preparing curriculum.
February	I will work with the faculty to identify the standards we need for assessments by examining what other countries are doing, what our universities and employers expect from students, and what experts in our field are recommending.
March	I will work with the faculty to prepare a draft of new standards for assessments that will serve as a framework for the teachers and leaders to follow when selecting and preparing assessments for students.
April	I will work with the faculty to identify the standards we need for instruction by examining what other countries are doing, what our universities and employers expect from students, and what experts in our field are recommending.
May	I will work with the faculty to prepare a draft of new standards for instruction that will serve as a framework for the teachers and leaders to follow when planning and executing instructional methods in the classroom.
June	I will bring the faculty to consensus on a new vision statement that is wrapped around specific standards expected in every classroom for the delivery of curriculum, assessments, and instruction.
July	I will work with teams of teachers to plan the next steps of implementing the new vision statement and adopted standards for curriculum, assessment, and instruction.

monthly planner (see Figures 9.6 and 9.7 on pages 101 and 102). Figures 9.8 and 9.9 on pages 103 and 104 show a typical daily calendar, but keep in mind that you will be using your own. Notice that the time allocation is during time outside of normal student contact hours. This is because the work does not involve direct contact with students or teachers. This is important to remember when scheduling actions. While most of the goals and actions required to improve your effectiveness can be scheduled during student contact hours, there will be ones that you will want to work on at other times (after school) in place of some of the traditional things you do (attending athletic events). Using the same example, the principal would schedule time during the school day when discussing the need for change, new vision for the school, and standards for the daily classroom.

Getting Into the Rhythm

By now you should be getting an understanding that the Tracker is both a conceptual framework as well as a planning device to improve your effectiveness in improving teaching and learning. You also might feel a little overwhelmed at this point as you consider setting goals, breaking them down into actions, and scheduling them into your daily planner. Goal setting is a skill, and the only way to get better is to practice. Most people are not accustomed to writing specific goals and setting action plans into place; but it has been my experience that principals who are successful in using this methodology do better when they think big, but start small. That being stated, it helps to see lots of examples, and that will be presented in the following chapters. For now, a general understanding of the system is all that is needed.

Getting Deeper into the Components of the Tracker

In the following chapters we will take a much closer look at each component and subcomponent of the Tracker. Each chapter will contain a number of resources that will be of value as you shift your daily time into effective leadership practices. Along with this, specific goals will be offered under each subcomponent to help you gain a clearer understanding of the specific types of activity that connect with leadership effectiveness.

Figure 9.6. Effective Principal Tracker—Monthly Plan

Month:

Week 1	Monthly Goal	Action	Time	Scheduled
Week 2	**Monthly Goal**	**Action**	**Time**	**Scheduled**
Week 3	**Monthly Goal**	**Action**	**Time**	**Scheduled**
Week 4	**Monthly Goal**	**Action**	**Time**	**Scheduled**

Figure 9.7. Effective Principal Tracker—Monthly Plan

Month: <u>August</u>

Week 1	Monthly Goal	Action	Time	Scheduled
	I will deepen my own understanding of the need to change.	☐ Study internal data	4 hrs.	✓

Week 2	Monthly Goal	Action	Time	Scheduled
	I will deepen my own understanding of the need to change.	☐ Study external data	4 hrs.	✓

Week 3	Monthly Goal	Action	Time	Scheduled
	I will deepen my own understanding of the need to change.	☐ Prepare outline	2 hrs.	✓

Week 4	Monthly Goal	Action	Time	Scheduled
	I will deepen my own understanding of the need to change.	☐ Prepare PowerPoint	3 hrs.	✓

Figure 9.8. Effective Principal Tracker—Daily Planner					
Daily Planner					
Time	**Monday**	**Tuesday**	**Wednesday**	**Thursday**	**Friday**
7:00–8:00					
8:00–9:00					
9:00–10:00					
10:00–11:00					
11:00–12:00					
12:00–1:00					
1:00–2:00					
2:00–3:00					
3:00–4:00					
4:00–5:00					
6:00–7:00					
7:00–8:00					

Figure 9.9. Effective Principal Tracker—Daily Planner					
Daily Planner					
Time	Monday	Tuesday	Wednesday	Thursday	Friday
7:00–8:00					
8:00–9:00					
9:00–10:00					
10:00–11:00					
11:00–12:00					
12:00–1:00					
1:00–2:00					
2:00–3:00					
3:00–4:00					
4:00–5:00	Need for change: Internet search		Need for change: Read chapter 8 of The World is Flat		
6:00–7:00	Need for change: Internet search			Need for change: Work on PowerPoint	
7:00–8:00					

Chapter 10

Setting and Shaping Expectations

America's future will be determined by the home and the school. The child becomes largely what he is taught; hence we must watch what we teach, and how we live.

—JANE ADDAMS

Setting and shaping expectations in an organization is the prime responsibility of leadership. In this chapter we will explore a variety of practices that principals can use to help teachers get back to their professional roots and embrace a common vision that reconnects with a passion for helping children. By establishing a strong sense of a need for change, principals can ignite a passion among the staff and engage people in a more thoughtful and natural approach to reaching agreement on what we should expect for all children each time they enter a classroom.

Rebuilding a Passion for Change

Think about how many times leaders have sent a group of teachers to a workshop, hoping that they would bring back great ideas that would somehow kindle a fire under their colleagues and bring about improvement. They returned with passionate ideas about how to improve teaching and learning, only to discover that the message was not embraced by those around them. Excited teachers realized that their best hope was to retreat to their classrooms and go it alone. Schools have invested a considerable amount of funds repeating this pattern over and over while nothing really changes. Schools would be better served by placing a moratorium on these expensive ventures and instead focusing on what they can do to get people excited about the importance of change.

Teachers are busy people, and simply introducing more stimuli for change will not connect with their work. They get a constant stream of flyers, e-mails, and advertising from a variety of educational promoters, many with good products and services but offering too much of the same approach to school improvement. I have yet to participate in a workshop that served up the magic bullet that produced lasting change. The reason is very clear. You can't initiate change in any form without dealing directly with the culture of the school. Whether it is a high-performing school or one that is struggling, change will not be achieved unless people see a clear and compelling reason to do so. Yet, too many times, leaders make the assumption that if they pronounce the need for improvement, or point out test scores that are less than acceptable, people will fall in line. The workshop circuit is not the answer. Neither is an influx of new programs.

What is missing in a school culture that does not embrace change is twofold. First, there is a lack of common understanding of the purpose of the daily work of the adults. This may sound strange but try it out. Ask a sample of teachers to articulate their purpose, and you will most certainly get a variety of answers. By the way, try this with school administrators and you will get similar results. Thus, when a change is introduced, the culture produces a wide variety of reactions that collide with one another.

Second, people don't see the need to change when the organization is satisfied with the status quo. Successful coaches know that celebrating a victory does not prepare you for the next contest. The job of the coach is to make sure that the team is not satisfied and that the culture remains focused on why everyone needs to change and improve. Too often schools become either satisfied with the results or uninterested in them. It is the job of leadership to get people back to their passions and connect these with a sense of urgency to improve.

Making the Case for Change

In the opening of this book we looked at the evolution of American schools in the context of a variety of variables that should cause school leaders to step back and realize the urgency for change in the ways we are preparing children for their futures. The data is overwhelming; yet we find many school cultures disconnected from the information that would cause people to respond with a passion to do what is right for kids. How do you get the culture of the school reconnected? Start with the faculty by giving them a presentation that opens the conversation and gives "legs" to a process that will build a high level of concern. I have found it useful to invest time in creating a PowerPoint that covers a variety of issues that schools should examine before embarking on a serious discussion of purpose and vision. It not only provides a means to get people talking but also allows you to build your own expertise on the topic of why we need to change schools.

It also helps to use stories and questions to ease into the topic. For example, if we asked coaches how they prepare their teams to compete, they would tell us that they utilize the following strategies:

- ◆ Scout the competition.
- ◆ Practice at least as much as the competition.
- ◆ Prepare the players to perform better than the competition.

Then present the following questions:

- ◆ Do we know how other countries are preparing their children for the future?
- ◆ Do we know the length of the school year of other countries?
- ◆ Do we know how well our students perform compared to students in other countries?

You probably will get limited responses or a stream of misperceptions such as:

"We don't need to compete, America is number one."
"Our methods of instruction are superior."
"We teach the whole child; they teach memorization."
"They don't teach all of the kids, just the smart ones."

These are all attempts to rationalize and resist change. The job of the leader is to present a lock step, ironclad case that is so powerful and overwhelming that it starts a lively debate and leads the audience to ask the question: "What can we do?"

Presenting the Need for Change

When you present the need for change to an audience, it is important to incorporate data and issues that are both internal as well as external to the school. The external data allows the audience to see that they are not the direct cause of these issues but need to pay attention to them. The internal data should include factors and results that are closer to home and more in control by the school. But keep in mind that people need to see both, because all point to a need to improve how we prepare children for a fast-changing world. Make sure that you cite each source of information directly on each slide. It is essential that the audience understands that you didn't make up the information or presented a biased point of view. You can decide the topics that you feel are relevant to the audience. Here are some of the ones I have found to be compelling to teachers and members of the school community:

External:
  ☐ Length of U.S. school year (180 days) vs. other countries (China = 251 days)
  ☐ Declining value of the high school diploma (in terms of wages)
  ☐ Performance of U.S. students in comparison to other countries
  ☐ Outsourcing of quality jobs overseas (engineering, etc.)
  ☐ Increasing poverty in the U.S. (one-third are children)

☐ Increasing disparity in income among the upper, middle, and lower classes
☐ Lack of rigor in schools
☐ Shortage of math and science majors in undergraduate programs
☐ Higher levels of broadband usage among populations in other countries
☐ Global competition and the declining value of low-skilled labor
☐ Shortage of scientists in critical fields
☐ Long-term educational plans of competing nations (China, India)

Internal:
☐ The gap between state achievement results and NAEP results
☐ The lack of rigor of state and local curriculum, standards, and assessments
☐ The percentage of students below the proficiency level on state assessments
☐ The dropout rate of the school
☐ The percentage of students that do not pursue education beyond high school

Passion is an emotion that can take many forms such as love, hate, fear, joy, grief, and anguish. Our goal in presenting the need for change is to ignite these feelings in order to move the culture of the school toward a clear vision and focused work. Some leaders believe that their role is to keep everyone calm and maintain a climate of satisfaction. Effective leaders do just the opposite. But what about keeping the passion alive? Don't these feeling drift away over time?

Sustaining a Passion for Change

One presentation will not be enough. To sustain a passion for change, principals must engage a variety of techniques to keep the discussions and dialogue going, so that the energy to change and improve gets recharged over and over. Some of the strategies that school leaders have employed include asking teachers to present one topic at each of the monthly faculty meetings, placing articles in teacher mailboxes, conducting book studies, inviting guest speakers, and sharing news reports on related topics. Remember that cultural change cannot take place through a single event, but rather through a sustained endeavor to bring people to a common understanding and a passion to respond.

The Quick Fix Syndrome

As you build a passion for change within the culture, some people will begin to suggest fixes to the challenges being presented. Schools have a tradition of reacting to symptoms of problems rather than the sources. For example, one of the greatest problems we face in public education is student performance on external audits (state assessment, standardized test) that measure learning in basic skills and subjects. We have attempted to address this issue by designing staff development or sending teachers to expensive workshops, when the source of the problem is not training as much as it is a continued practice of allowing teachers to perform their work in isolation of one another. Be careful with suggestions for quick fixes and instead use the passion that people display to drive them towards a clearer vision.

Focusing on Teaching and Learning

Many of the processes that schools use to create a vision begin with assembling a representative group of people (teachers, administrators, students, parents and community members) to come together and prepare a series of statements that reflect what the school should become. Some include role expectations while others lay out philosophical statements of an ideal campus. Everyone has an equal voice and at some point in the process a consensus of opinion is reached.

The shortcoming of this approach is that it does not reflect what we know from the research about student learning. Once students arrive on campus, the greatest determinant of their achievement will be the teachers to whom they are assigned. The real work of schools takes place in classrooms between teachers and students. Thus, when creating a vision for a school, teachers must be the starting point for this process and have the greatest amount of input. Would a hospital begin their visioning process with a representative group of community members to decide what needs to take place in order to provide effective health care? Should all constituents have an equal voice in the practices and procedures that will be employed to educate children? This is not to say that the input of others is not important. It is more a question of the degree of influence and the importance of trusting those with the greatest expertise to shape the vision. Schools have routinely created vision and mission statements that disconnect from the most important providers in the school—teachers.

A Better Way to Create a School Vision

As teachers get more familiar with the plethora of issues that should cause schools to change, it is a great opportunity to refocus the vision of the school on an important question:

What do we want every student to experience in their daily learning in every classroom?

By asking this question, teachers can embrace a visioning process that wraps around the classroom and empowers them to identify the conditions of teaching and learning that need to take place. The pillars for the vision need to be established around the three elements of curriculum, assessment, and instruction that in combination produce the daily learning experiences for each child. An easy place to begin is to present the faculty with the question we have raised and ask them to work in teams to respond by identifying descriptors under each of the three elements of the classroom.

What do we want?

Before starting this exercise we need to discuss the role of the leader in shaping a vision. Contrary to what you may have learned, leaders should never begin the discussion of vision prior to knowing where they want to go. Too often, leaders think that the visioning process is about consensus of opinion. Visioning requires the leader to first determine the vision for the school using the best available knowledge and information, and then guide the organization toward a discovery process that brings people to a similar conclusion. Where does the vision come from? It comes from a clear understanding of present and future conditions. Thus, the work that the leaders do in pulling together data and information on the need for change will point towards the path that must be taken. Let's take a look at how this plays out in the vision of a classroom using curriculum, assessment, and instruction as the three reference points. By now you have probably noticed the order in which I have referenced these. I saved instruction as the last consideration of the three, based on Wiggins and McTighe's Backward Design Process that was introduced in their book, *Understanding by Design* (1998). Their backward design process suggested that educators sequence their planning by starting with identified results, then determining evidence of results, and finally planning instruction (curriculum, assessment, instruction).

Figure 10.1 displays some of the descriptors that define a vision that emanates from what a school should expect in each classroom. The descriptors should address the symptoms and problems presented in the need for change and serve as the cornerstones for standards to be achieved.

Figure 10.1. Defining the Vision		
Symptoms from Need for Change Presentations	⇨ **Problem** ⇨	**Vision Descriptor**
Curriculum: ■ Competing nations introduce subjects such as algebra and geometry at earlier ages ■ State standards are set at minimum levels ■ Entry-level jobs in trades require higher skills than in the past	■ State curriculums fail to reflect comparable knowledge and skills that children in other countries are learning ■ State and local curriculums tend to focus on basic knowledge and skills ■ State and local curriculums fail to reach the knowledge and skills necessary for today's workforce training requirements	International Rigorous Workforce Ready
Assessment: ■ Teachers construct assessments in isolation of each other ■ State assessments are low level ■ Teacher assessments fail to accurately measure student learning	■ Schools lack common assessments based on standards ■ State assessments tend to measure basic skills instead of proficiency ■ Teachers have minimal training in test/assessment construction	Common Formatives Rigorous Summatives Valid and Reliable
Instruction: ■ Instruction continues to be one size fits all ■ Students are bored with classroom instruction ■ Students complain about the lack of relevance in their learning	■ Students learn at different rates ■ Students are being raised in a culture of technology that provides high levels of engagement and instant feedback ■ Classroom instruction is disconnected from the world of students	Differentiated Engaging Authentic

⇩

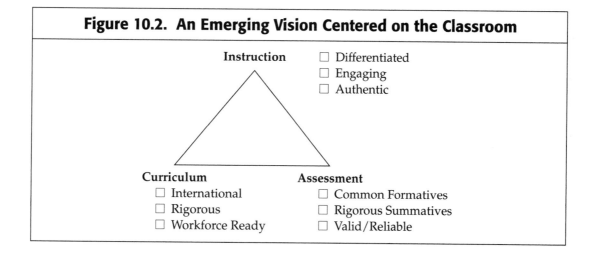

Figure 10.2. An Emerging Vision Centered on the Classroom

Instruction
☐ Differentiated
☐ Engaging
☐ Authentic

Curriculum
☐ International
☐ Rigorous
☐ Workforce Ready

Assessment
☐ Common Formatives
☐ Rigorous Summatives
☐ Valid/Reliable

While your own descriptors will vary, you will discover that if you lead a room full of teachers through the same process, you will get surprisingly similar results. Why? Because the majority of our teachers are knowledgeable of what really needs to happen in classrooms. We don't empower them to articulate this vision, nor do we provide them with the resources and time to pursue it. What if you notice that pieces of the vision are missing when you engage them? Have key questions ready that will move people toward your vision:

Curriculum

- What kind of curriculum do we want to have in order to ensure that our children are getting the same knowledge and skills that kids in competing nations are getting?
- What kind of curriculum do we want to have so that children are challenged beyond the basic level skills presented in the state standards?
- What kind of curriculum do we want to have so that every child graduates with the necessary knowledge and skills to continue their education in college or workforce training?

Assessment

- What kind of assessments do we need to inform teachers so that immediate adjustments can be made for students not reaching mastery level?
- What kind of assessments do we need to measure student learning that goes beyond the basic level knowledge and skills of the state testing process?
- What kind of assessments do we need to ensure that we are accurately measuring the objectives of our local curriculum?

Instruction

- What kind of instruction do we need knowing that each child has unique learning needs and styles?
- What kind of instruction do we need knowing that teachers must compete for the attention of children who are growing up in a culture of technology that provides highly engaging activities with instant feedback?
- What kind of instruction do we need knowing that many children do not see the relevance of the learning being required in classrooms?

Putting Definition to the Vision

Once there is consensus on the vision it is important to continue with collaborative discussions that put greater definition to each of the descriptors. Eventually, a clear picture of the standards to be developed around each corner of the triangle will emerge. For example, if we use the descriptors from Figure 10.1 under instruction, the subheadings might look like the following:

Differentiated
- ☐ Content
- ☐ Process
- ☐ Assessment

Engaging
- ☐ Quick feedback
- ☐ Hands on
- ☐ Challenging

Authentic
- ☐ Connected to real word
- ☐ Applied to daily skills
- ☐ Relevant to the future

Notice that each of the subheadings contribute to not only a deeper understanding of the standard, but also opportunities for teacher collaboration in the creation and refinement of the standards. Deepening the vision is an exciting process that empowers teachers to discover, collaborate, and plan around what is most important to them, the classroom.

Strengthening Relationships

Strong relationships are founded on covenants and commitments, not titles, positions, or transactions. The principal's role in relationship building is to shape them around the vision of the school so that people work together for a common purpose.

Teachers are in a position to be the primary salespeople of the vision and the builders of strong relationships throughout the school community. Using a visioning process that empowers teachers to reach out and engage other stakeholders in further development of the school's vision allows them to shape a school culture that keeps teaching and learning at the center. The principal can lead teachers in a process to identify exactly what they need from each stakeholder group in order to make the vision become a reality. Their responses will vary, but some of the common ones will look like the following:

Stakeholders	What Teachers Need from Stakeholders
From students:	✓ Come to school prepared to learn ✓ Be attentive and on task in class ✓ Complete all homework
From parents:	✓ Send your child prepared to learn ✓ Become involved in your child's learning ✓ Communicate with your child's teacher

From principals:
- ✓ Provide time for collaborative work
- ✓ Be visible in classrooms and team meetings
- ✓ Protect instructional time from distractions

From central office:
- ✓ Give our campus the autonomy to fulfill the vision
- ✓ Respect the culture and uniqueness of our school
- ✓ Provide the resources we need

From the community:
- ✓ Support academics as the first priority
- ✓ Relieve the school of programs designed to solve social issues
- ✓ Provide the resources we need

Whatever their expectations become, it is important that teachers have the opportunity to identify the types of support they will need in order to deliver the vision of the classroom.

These expectations can serve as a means of developing stronger and healthier relationships that reestablish a bond between teachers and the stakeholders who owe their commitment and support to the work of the classroom.

Professional Learning Communities

Much has been written about the importance of establishing conditions that enable teachers to learn and share together in the essential work of schools. Yet, many schools have jumped into the implementation of professional learning communities without taking into consideration the cultural changes that need to occur in order to move teachers from isolated work to collaborative endeavors. Many principals underestimate the time that is required to work with teachers and coach them through the basics of successful teamwork. Others are surprised how different the chemistry of each team can be and the varying needs for intervention and guidance. The formula for effective work of each learning community includes the following:

Effective Teams = Focused work on the vision + Established team behaviors
(improvements to the triangle) (healthy team relationships)

As principals transition more of their time into classrooms, it will be equally important to invest time attending meetings of teachers and helping them improve their collaborative skills. Leading authors on the processes of establishing professional learning communities recommend that teachers establish rules and norms for getting along and conducting work in a manner that is respectful of one another (DuFour & Eaker). Others such as Patrick Lencioni (2002) suggested that all teams exhibit five types of dysfunctions that must be addressed in order to build healthy relationships and effective shared learning and practice:

Lencioni's Five Dysfunctions of a Team
Absence of Trust
Fear of Conflict
Lack of Commitment
Avoidance of Accountability
Inattention to Results

Lencioni provided a useful model and resources to help leaders guide teams through each dysfunction and rotate them from weaknesses to strengths. There are also a variety of instruments that a principal can bring to teachers to help them measure their team skills and work on improving the quality of their relationships. Appendix D displays a survey that helps to measure each member's perception of the degree to which the team models attributes of a professional learning community identified in the literature. Appendix E includes a list of other tools that are helpful to measure team behaviors.

Stakeholders

Principals are challenged with a multitude of stakeholders, all with needs, interests, and agenda that at times can be overwhelming. After juggling these challenges for many years it finally dawned on me that each had certain "hot buttons," and that as long as I took care of these most of the other issues were less important. I also discovered that if I took the initiative to develop these relationships around the vision for the school, most people would jump at the opportunity to help.

Listed below are some of the key strategies that I found useful to employ in developing strong relationships with stakeholders:

Central Office	☐ Keep them informed of critical events and information
	☐ Ask for support to help the school reach the vision
	☐ Provide periodic progress reports on work towards the vision
Parents	☐ Make a personal commitment to help each child succeed
	☐ Strengthen communication channels between home and school
	☐ Provide them with resources to engage in their child's learning
Community	☐ Meet with key leaders and discuss mutual issues
	☐ Pitch them projects that will support the vision of the school
	☐ Give them public recognition for their support
Students	☐ Use frequent visits to classrooms to connect with students
	☐ Ask students about the quality of their classroom experiences
	☐ Follow up on student concerns about the school

Remember that part of the 360° feedback that you collected (chapter 4) includes stakeholder perceptions of your leadership and can serve as a good source of areas for improving relationships.

Setting High Expectations

One of the most important roles of the principal is to set high expectations for teaching and learning so that the work of the school lifts all human beings to a level they are capable of accomplishing. Part of the investigative work of the need for change will reveal the importance of ratcheting up standards so that the targets will enable all children to acquire the knowledge and skills necessary to go on with their training and education beyond high school.

High Academic Standards

There has been considerable debate over setting a high bar for students and some continue to argue that doing so will cause stress, unhappy children and higher dropout rates. Evidence of this is almost nonexistent. Experts on stress contend that all of us need some of it because it drives us to achieve (Wein, 2000). When national studies of school dropouts have been conducted (Bridgeland, Dilulio & Morison, 2006), the leading reasons for doing so have centered on boredom and lack of relevance, not high standards. Happiness is relative. Are we looking for immediate gratification or intrinsic satisfaction that comes from a sustained struggle? Effective principals set high targets and lead adults in helping each student reach them.

States tend to write curriculum standards that reflect minimum expectations, and therefore fall short of the rigor necessary to stretch the learning of children to the levels that would be considered equivalent to those practiced in other countries. Some states, such as South Carolina, have aligned their standards similar to those assessed by the NAEP. But for the most part, schools are handed a set of documents that contain learning objectives that are vague and written at the bottom of Bloom's Taxonomy. This leaves local school districts and school campuses with a false sense of what a quality curriculum should resemble. Some countries like Singapore offer their standards for others to view on their website (http://www.moe.gov.sg). Providing these to teachers will help them see the standards being used by their colleagues in other countries. Other rigorous curriculums such as the Advanced Placement Program and International Baccalaureate Program represent high standards that can be articulated throughout a K–12 program.

Targets are also derived from the assessments that schools put in place. Again, states are notorious for developing criterion-referenced tests that measure basic knowledge and skills and rarely get to a level that measures proficiency. In addition, cut scores are set so that a majority of students are identified as "passing" and thus violate the concept of measuring mastery. Principals can ratchet up expectations by engaging the faculty in the review of external audits (such as nationally standardized tests) that do a more effective job of measuring rigor and proficiency. Effective schools administer their own standardized tests to supplement the state assessments in order to set higher expectations, and get a more accurate read on the performance of their students. Principals of secondary schools have established the practice of giving the ACT or SAT to an entire grade level as a means of setting higher standards for performance and measuring the readiness of students for college studies and workforce training.

Daily instruction must engage children in work that identifies their starting point and scales them up to higher levels of learning. Research on the impact of instruction has revealed that many educators teach to the middle of the class and leave underachievers behind, while holding advanced learners back (Sanders & Rivers, 1997). Principals can monitor this issue by conducting regular walk-throughs of classrooms to determine if all children are being taught at appropriate levels that provide significant rigor and stretch.

Tracker Goals for Your Consideration: Setting and Shaping Expectations

Need for Change:

I will . . .
1. Study the internal and external factors for change and make a presentation (e.g., PowerPoint) to the faculty.
2. Coordinate discussions, book studies, presentations by teachers and distribution of timely articles to maintain a sense of urgency in the school culture.

Focus on Teaching and Learning:

I will . . .
1. Engage the faculty in a visioning process to identify standards for curriculum, assessment, and instruction.
2. Empower the faculty to share their expectations of stakeholders in reaching the vision of the school.

Strengthening Relationships:

I will . . .
1. Provide assistance to teachers to improve their teamwork skills and relationships with each other.
2. Work with stakeholders to strengthen their support of the vision of the school.

Setting High Expectations:

I will . . .
1. Work directly with the faculty to set high academic standards for all children.
2. Engage the faculty in the design of curriculum, assessment, and instruction that provide students with globally competitive skills.

Chapter 11

Creating Disequilibrium

Great necessities call out great virtues.

—ABIGAIL ADAMS

Effective leaders understand that a high level of satisfaction among members of an organization signal the danger of complacency. High performance schools embody a culture of dissatisfaction with results and relentless pursuit of improvement. In this chapter we will examine the role of the principal in modeling and managing change for the purpose of improving teaching and learning throughout the school. Change involves the alteration of structures and processes, but most importantly, modifications of behavior. Effective principals model these behaviors and then manage them through key people who will advance the vision of the school.

Modeling Change

Leaders cannot ask people to do things that they would not do themselves. I will never forget a principal I knew who created a seating chart for faculty so that maximum control was maintained during all school assemblies in the gymnasium. Two thousand teenagers could be quite intimidating, especially on a Friday afternoon before a big football game. Yet, it was well known among teachers that the principal would retreat to his office during the assembly. He was afraid of the kids and didn't want to be tested by them in full view of the faculty. He preached discipline and order, yet on many occasions would differentiate consequences for students, depending on the influence of their parents in the community. There was no personal commitment. This not only damaged his leadership, but also caused the culture of the school to be highly resistant to any changes he suggested.

Clarifying Your Expectations

People want to know what their leaders expect. This can be a tricky path to walk because some want to know specifics, while others just need to hear the belief system of the leaders so they can understand the direction the culture will be taking. This is a common phenomenon in many schools. Leaders can create conditions that support change by clarifying what they value and signaling the direction they want to take. Telling people what you stand for and what you want the school to become helps people sort through the multitude of mixed signals they have experienced over the years.

People who have operated in an autocratic culture are accustomed to leadership that is more specific and directive, yet less effective. If you have ever inherited a culture like this you have experienced people asking permission to perform numerous actions that require little thought. They don't see themselves as part of the decision-making process, and therefore specificity is very important to them. They also take no ownership in the results of the organization and are quick to blame leadership. While most school cultures are not this extreme, many involve a mix of people who want specific direction and those who want participation in the decision-making process.

The balance that leaders must create in clarifying their expectations is to convey a short list of beliefs along with a personal vision that gives people direction, yet holds back specificity so that people anticipate empowerment and involvement in decision making.

How can principals convey their beliefs and personal vision? Take a lesson from public and corporate leaders, who rely on talking points to help them stick to a consistent message that expresses what they want, and what they expect. Figure 11.1 displays a sample of a framework that could be used for discussions and written communications to clarify the expectations of a leader. While your own personal statements will vary, the example provides clarity and balance, as well as a signal that the leader invites continuous participation in the decision making and work of the school. Keep it simple; keep it clear.

Figure 11.1. Sample Framework of a Principal's Values and Vision

What I Value:
→ A school where adults put the interests of students first and do everything they can do to ensure that each student succeeds in his or her learning.
→ Relationships that are built on shared covenants, rather than titles, positions, or transactions.
→ A belief that school is a place where all people learn, create knowledge and skills, and improve the quality of life.

My Vision:
My vision for our school is to continuously engage stakeholders in looking at variables that impact the futures of our students and use their passion to drive collaborative work to ensure ongoing improvement to curriculum, assessment, and instruction, so that each member of the school learns and grows accordingly.

Effective leaders talk about their beliefs and personal vision with every opportunity that comes along. They understand that schools are busy places and that most adults work in isolation and have few opportunities to have reflective discussions with colleagues. Faculty meetings, lunchroom conversations, and informal contacts are all important forums for the principal to deepen an understanding of what is expected and the vision that will define the path of the school.

Modifying Your Behaviors

As you clarify your expectations and vision for the school, people will be watching to see if you mean what you say. Those who are accustomed to an autocratic style will continue to ask permission, and others who are waiting to be invited to participate will look to the next big decision and how you will handle it. Leaders can model what they want by changing their own behaviors in ways that change perceptions and begin to shift the culture towards the intended vision.

Sometimes small changes can send big messages. For example, in many schools, the principal's secretary is the gatekeeper for all of the teacher supplies. I once inherited a principalship where these items were kept in a locked vault, and teachers had to beg the secretary on a regular basis for a small allotment of paper, markers, and scissors. Sound familiar? After announcing to the faculty that I wanted a school where all adults would be treated as professionals, I started with a small change that, unanticipated by me, would become huge in terms of perception. I asked the secretary to divide all of the supplies equally among the faculty and have the custodian deliver these to their classrooms. This started the shift. They wanted more and waited in anticipation. Next was the suspension of turning in lesson plans. At a faculty meeting, I announced that I was not interested in looking over teachers' shoulders or personally judging their lessons, but rather would expect that each teacher would always have in place a daily plan that reflected their best effort to reach each child. You could almost feel the earth move.

As you roll out expectations, it is critical to reflect on those practices both large and small that will serve as indicators of your intentions to walk the talk. Some of these will be obvious, while others may be so small that they will escape your attention. For this reason as well as others, it is wise to gather a coalition of teachers who are supportive of your vision and trustworthy in sharing their views. They will be able to point out past practices that teachers consider autocratic and inform you of what is being shared among the faculty as you move the culture forward.

Perhaps the greatest means of modeling what you want is to have the faculty see you doing it, right out of the gate. If you want the focus of the vision of the school to be wrapped around the classroom, then it is imperative to be present frequently in classrooms. This means scheduling it and doing it each day, every day, especially toward the beginning of a new endeavor to move the school toward a focus on teaching and learning. It is also important that when visiting classrooms, you refrain from invoking the old norms and instead employ new processes that reflect new standards. In chapter 13, we will discuss the practice of using classroom walk-throughs as a means of supporting and coaching quality instruction versus evaluating teachers.

The same holds true for engagement of teachers before, during, and after school hours to discuss important work in curriculum, assessment, and instruction. Principals who want teachers to collaborate to improve classrooms must be directly involved in the work to provide support, participate as a colleague, and guide people through unfamiliar territory. Too often, when embarking on the creation of a collaborative culture, principals assume that serving up a measured amount of authority and responsibility to teachers will be enough to convince them of their intent. But nothing drives it home more than rolling up your sleeves, and sharing the tough conversations, discussions, and work that need to take place.

Effective leaders also model giving up comfortable, traditional, and familiar practices so that the organization can benefit. Principals take comfort in doing those things that are simple, routine, and visible to all. But as we discussed in earlier chapters, many of these contribute little to improved teaching and learning. Letting go of these, signals that a change is taking place and that the principal is personally willing to do whatever it takes to reach the vision of the school. Not being seen in the office, cafeteria, or on bus duty on a daily basis causes people to wonder where you are. Eventually they will come to understand, and expect that you can be found in classrooms, meetings with teachers, and conversations with students and staff.

Modifying Structures and Processes

Change is painful, and for administrators, altering structures and processes can border on the unthinkable. Consider the following statements that I have heard school administrators make when it comes to changing systems and processes that are in place:

"I'm supportive of this idea of professional learning communities as long as I don't have to change the schedule."

"If you allow teachers to participate in the selection of new staff, they will expect you to pick their favorite candidate."

"Allowing teachers to refine the curriculum will only get me in trouble with central office."

"Changing procedures will cost me extra work and make my secretary unhappy."

"I believe in collaboration, but aren't there some decisions that are mine alone?"

Principals must be willing to make radical changes to structures and processes if there is any hope of shifting the culture and bringing about meaningful change. This requires leaders to give up control and place extra time into those areas that knowingly will cause short-term frustration for themselves and their office staff. But as coaches affirm, the pain is worth the gain.

One of the most significant issues that a principal faces when asking teachers to collaborate on a regular basis is that of time embedded in the school day to meet. For most schools, this means changing the daily schedule, altering teaching assignments, reorganizing student schedules, modifying the lunch periods, and reassigning room utilization. Yet, without doing so, any effort to promote teacher collaboration will succumb to resistance and push back from the culture. Structures cannot be sacred when modeling change for the organization. Many principals have discovered that refined innovations such as block scheduling have not only enabled the culture to implement learning communities, but also realize benefits that are congruent with the desired changes of the school. For example, schools that have adopted block schedules have reduced the number of class changes, and in turn, behavior issues that typically occur during these times. Other benefits include the elimination of study halls, increased time that students can accumulate credits towards graduation, and improved access to classes that previously were unavailable. Leaders have to model a willingness to let go of existing structures and examine alternative ones that will support the direction they want the school to take.

The same can be said for processes that are deeply entrenched in the school, but get in the way of a new vision. Processes require policy and procedures to integrate them into the organization and thus, leaders are reluctant to change them. But again, it will be counterproductive to the culture of the school if the leader chooses status quo, when it comes to work that will cost personal time and effort. This is not to say that the principal must relinquish processes to collaborative decisions that will cause major disruption to the school. Principals must find an appropriate balance between the changes desired, and the need to maintain authority and responsibility for the results of the organization. For example, it is important to involve teachers in the selection of new staff. Teachers can provide valuable input, especially when they are focused on identifying potential colleagues who share the same values, commitments, knowledge, and skills, that are congruent with the vision of the school. The principal can find an appropriate balance by sharing authority and responsibility, without giving up the final decision to reject or hire a potential candidate. By setting the parameter that teacher input will be limited to the identification of strengths and weaknesses of each candidate, the principal can share the selection process in a manner that is consistent with the vision, yet respectful of the ultimate accountability of the principal to the school and the district.

Modeling behaviors that demonstrate a leader's willingness to change, is vital to a healthy organization. It is imperative for principals to understand that teachers and other members of the school community will judge them by the way they behave. It doesn't take long for the word to go out when people witness personal acts of the principal that signal a commitment to change. When this happens, it is time to turn to the other members of the school culture, and ask them to do the same. As leaders push their organization to change, it will be important to manage it in ways that keeps the culture aligned to the vision.

Managing Change

Managing change in an organization requires a considerable amount of skill and conscious effort to massage the culture, encourage risk taking, protect the vision, alter perceptions, and provide positive feedback to those who model behaviors and actions that contribute to the organizational goals. In fact, writers such as Michael Fullan (2001) have made the case that change cannot be controlled, but rather led. The complexity of variables that come into play whenever changes are introduced should cause leaders to understand that a state of disequilibrium is necessary if people are going to experiment and improve. The role of the principal is to facilitate and guide the school so that the culture can move away from old norms and values that hold back the transformation of the school.

The Principal as Facilitator of Change

Change causes things to be in flux, and the principal must get people comfortable with the notion that ambiguity is a natural product of a culture that is in transition. As old structures and processes are being disassembled and new ones being designed, it will cause people to cling to the familiar or beg for specificity and direction. Whenever I heard someone repeatedly ask for my expectations, it was a red flag that the individual was fearful of taking a risk and being on the line in front of others. We have all heard people say, "Just tell me what to do." Effective leaders resist these questions by asking people for their input and ideas. This will cause frustration in the short run, but in the long run, will push the organization towards valuing experimentation and innovation.

The principal will also need to facilitate similar behaviors among teacher leaders so that they too encourage growth. Remember that teachers have operated under top down management styles for decades, and therefore, when given the opportunity to lead will model old leadership styles unless the principal intervenes and facilitates a growth in their skills. Teacher leadership training is essential to the change process in schools and is an important investment of time.

It is equally essential for principals to analyze the subcultures within the school and facilitate change accordingly. As teachers are organized into teams to collaborate on important work, the principal should avoid using a one-size-fits-all checklist approach to helping them identify goals, design strategies, and experiment with new approaches. For example, instead of marching the entire staff through improvements to the curriculum at the same time, allow teams to determine their greatest opportunities for change and improvement. Some may decide that their greatest weakness is in the daily assessment of children's skill sets. Don't force a change. Facilitate it in ways that model respect and trust.

Finally, change invariably carries risk. Principals must facilitate a level of trust by ensuring that they will not be quick to judge or expect immediate results. Change is a process that takes time and sustained effort. Don't cut it short by getting out the yardstick, and declaring victories or defeats before the results are in.

Using the Vision as a Filter for Change

Years ago, one of my best mentors sat me down and reviewed the vision of the school I was about to lead. He explained that it was formed through a collaborative process and that it represented a common set of beliefs that served as the foundation for every major decision and change initiated in the culture of the school. He went on to state that I had the opportunity to alter the vision, but would have to present a compelling case that would be filtered through the beliefs in place. It was a great lesson that helped me understand the importance of vision, and the role of leadership, in protecting it. The principal is the keeper of the vision.

Throughout the process of change, people will suggest a variety of innovative and experimental strategies that alter the structures and processes of the school. The role of the principal is to ensure that people reach consensus using the vision as the target for each initiative being proposed. If a decision escapes this parameter, it is the responsibility of leadership to step in and, first, raise questions in real time settings that redirect people back on track without invoking a veto. But if a veto is necessary, the principal must have the courage to use it. Figure 11.2 provides some examples of good intentions that stray from the vision of a school, along with questions that a principal can use, to redirect the focus of the proposal back to the vision.

Managing Perceptions

Change is more about people rather than structures and processes. Therefore, it is important for the principal to be deeply involved, in gathering information on how the culture reacts and embraces perceptions that either move the school forward or detract from the progress to be made. Managing perceptions can be tricky. Some would argue that leaders should not concern themselves with perceptions, but when trying to move and shape a culture it is imperative to deal with them swiftly and directly. Ignoring these will empower

| Figure 11.2. Getting the Vision Back on Track with Questions ||
Proposal	Question
■ A group of teachers believe that some of the objectives of the curriculum are developmentally inappropriate for some students and therefore want to remove them for the entire grade level.	■ How does this proposal align with our vision of providing a rigorous curriculum that teachers can differentiate within a classroom?
■ A team of science teachers decides that students would be better served by providing three levels of each subject and assigning those not capable of going to college to a lower track.	■ How does this proposal align with our vision of providing all students with skills that allow them to select to go to college or workforce training programs?
■ Teachers have concluded that six-week grading periods are too short of a time span to accumulate enough assignments for determining a grade for each student, and therefore want to change to a nine-week grading period.	■ How does this proposal align with our vision of providing ongoing feedback to students and parents regarding progress towards learning?
■ Teachers are frustrated with student tardiness and want the school to suspend students when they have been late to school more than five times in a semester.	■ How does this proposal align with our vision of having parents support our need to get students to practice good attendance?
■ Teachers want to reorganize the time schedule in order to provide flexible time to students who are struggling in core subjects. Elective teachers are offended that some children will be missing their classes, on days when they need more learning time in core subjects. They plan to block the proposal.	■ How does this proposal align with our vision of differentiating the processes that teachers should use to ensure mastery of each learning objective?

those opposed to change, and stall efforts to improve the school. Perceptions can also hurt or disrupt the changes that teacher leaders are attempting to advance, and without the intervention of the principal, can discourage continued involvement.

Some principals use e-mails and web pages to post timely responses to rumors and misinformation. If the source of the information is revealed, it is important to talk to the individuals and give them the opportunity to be heard and to come to a clarification. If the perception is significant, don't wait. Call an emergency meeting of the faculty, and get in front of the issue before it festers.

As changes are rolled out, it is an important time to discuss beliefs. Many schools identify their belief system through a formal process, similar to the traditional approach to creating a vision. A traditional approach is to bring a representative group of people together to reach consensus on a formal set of beliefs. The beliefs are adopted as the foundation for all future actions of the school organization.

Not all people connect with this method, because they need to see examples and applications of the belief system. For this reason, it makes more sense to first get a vision in place, using the previous process described in chapter 10, and wait to identify beliefs as new structures and processes are proposed and designed to improve the school. In other words, beliefs can more easily be determined while pursuing a vision, rather than in advance of taking actions. It also is easier to test and clarify beliefs when multiple innovations are being proposed and implemented. Beliefs can be solidified as people reveal their thoughts and actions, so be patient before formalizing them. It is the vision that drives change.

Identify a Guiding Coalition

John Kotter (1996) suggested that when proposing change, leaders should identify a guiding coalition of those in the organization who are influential, both formal and informal. Schlechty (2001) added that it is important to include people who have the technical expertise to lead specific areas targeted for change. Since a majority of the changes we are discussing involve improvements to teaching and learning, the principal's guiding coalition should consist of teachers who understand the vision, and have the skills to lead collaborative work in curriculum, assessment, and instruction. Some will need assistance with leadership skills that strengthen their ability to influence others. Others will require ongoing reassurance that their leadership is critical to the vision of the school.

Of equal importance is the use of the guiding coalition to help the principal identify potential issues and problems as proposed changes emerge throughout the school. The coalition can help filter ideas through the vision, dispel rumors and misperceptions, ask questions that help to redirect proposals, and support the overall hard work of changing the culture.

Teachers who join the faculty during the change process will need special attention. Many schools use the days before school opens to put new teachers through a rigorous schedule of computer training, policy and procedures, human resource information, and meetings with the personnel department. A guiding coalition can be useful in redesigning new teacher orientation by first postponing the traditional training sessions to later in the year. New teachers need two things to jump-start them into a successful entry into the school culture. First, they need the basic survival kit of knowledge and skills that will enable them to get through the opening days and weeks of school. Second, they need a good introduction to the vision and culture of the school. Everyone knows how new teachers are pulled aside by veterans, some with good intentions, and others who want to advance their own agenda. The guiding coalition should be entrusted to familiarize new teachers with the important changes being pursued by the school and the expectations that have been identified for each classroom.

Rewards and Accolades that Encourage Change

Recognizing and rewarding work that is focused on changes that move the school towards the vision is essential. Teachers tend to shy away from public recognition that appears to be invented. Giving plaques, balloon bouquets, and other artifacts can be well intended, but it has been my experience that recognition on a personal and private level is received more positively by professionals. Effective principals notice many of the daily acts of risk taking and courage that teachers use to improve their classrooms. Notes of encouragement and simple e-mails at the end of a workday that convey, "I noticed that ...," carry a larger reward for those who are trying hard, but don't want to be singled out at a faculty meeting. Teachers just want to know that you noticed their efforts and support their continued attempts to innovate and improve. You can find additional ideas and resources in Kouzes & Posner's, *Encouraging the Heart: A Leader's Guide to Rewarding and Recognizing Others* (2003).

Finally, principals can also encourage change by rewarding people with intangibles that send a message that their efforts to go the extra mile for kids deserve special treatment. I know of many principals who bend the rules for faculty who need to leave work early or come in late to handle personal emergencies or family priorities. These simple acts leave long-lasting impressions that solidify a mutual commitment between the principal and the staff.

Tracker Goals for Your Consideration: Creating Disequilibrium

Modeling Change:

I will ...
1. Model change by revealing my personal values and vision for the school so that faculty understands the path to be followed.
2. Model change through behaviors that demonstrate a commitment to changing my daily practices to align with the vision of the school.
3. Model change by demonstrating a willingness to change structures and processes that support the vision of the school.

Managing Change:

I will . . .

1. Manage change by facilitating a culture in which teachers can experiment and innovate without fear of failure or pressure for results.
2. Manage change by asking key questions that realign proposed changes with the vision of the school.
3. Manage change by reacting to misperceptions and rumors with timely communication and direct engagement with key people.
4. Manage change by organizing and empowering a guiding coalition to advance the vision of the district.
5. Manage change by providing personal accolades and rewards to those who demonstrate risk taking and innovative work aligned with the vision of the school.

Chapter 12

Engaging Staff in Knowledge Transfer

If your actions inspire others to dream more, learn more, do more and become more, you are a leader.

—JOHN QUINCY ADAMS

Getting people to share best practices is one of the most underestimated and underutilized sources of improvement on school campuses. Many of the successful approaches used by teachers remain within the confines of their classrooms, in spite of attempts to implement a collaborative culture though the introduction of professional learning communities and other transformative endeavors. Transferring best practices to others requires much more than organizing teachers into teams and asking them to share with one another. It takes an understanding of the processes that are associated with knowledge transfer. In this chapter, we will borrow from the work of leaders in the field of knowledge management to lay out a practical approach for principals to use in helping their schools create and distribute best practices in the improvement of curriculum, assessment, and instruction.

Knowledge Transfer

Since the early 1970s companies have studied and successfully implemented the fundamentals of identifying effective practices and distributing this information to other employees who can use it to replicate desired results. It involves a serious appreciation of the knowledge that people create and a systematic effort to capture it. Knowledge management ensures that organizations pay attention to the infrastructures that successfully identify, collect, and deliver timely best practices to those people who can integrate them and improve performance.

To understand how a principal can effectively facilitate this process, we need to first examine the types of knowledge that exist, and how they get distributed. Knowledge can be presented in two forms: *explicit* and *tacit* (Nonaka). Explicit knowledge is information that is passed through formal processes, such as written documents and electronic sources. Tacit knowledge is the informal, practical information that exists within an organization that is difficult to express and to transfer between members (Nonaka & Takeuchi). The work of transferring tacit knowledge of best practices is the key to the knowledge transfer process. Figure 12.1 displays the generally accepted steps of knowledge transfer that successful organizations achieve, so that good ideas and successful processes are shared in a timely manner. Let's take a look at how the principal can use these steps to create and strengthen a culture of shared knowledge and practice to improve teaching and learning across the school organization.

Finding Best Practices

When we talk about finding best practices we are not referring to a workshop, commercial product, or Internet source. These are explicit sources of knowledge that reside outside of the school. What we want to find are the great ideas and effective practices that exist within a school that are used by individual teachers, partnerships, and teams to get successful results. We have all witnessed some of the most interesting and engaging lessons that excite students. Many of them go unnoticed by others, and therefore the potential benefits are lost.

What defines a best practice? Experts in the field of knowledge transfer tell us that best practices *are those acts that successfully achieve a specific focus of the organization.* Thus, we will use the vision of the school as our point of reference

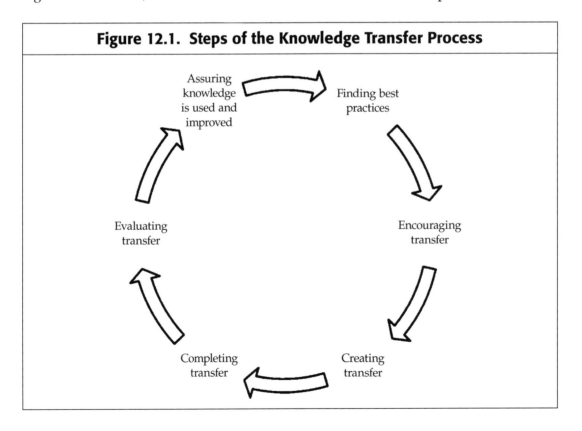

Figure 12.1. Steps of the Knowledge Transfer Process

Assuring knowledge is used and improved

Finding best practices

Evaluating transfer

Encouraging transfer

Completing transfer

Creating transfer

in locating best practices in curriculum, assessment, and instruction that produce improved learning for children.

Best practices bring best results. For this reason, a good starting place is to work backwards from the results of effective teachers and teams of teachers. By analyzing data from state assessments, standardized tests, and common assessments, principals can accumulate a list of successful teachers, partnerships, and teams that have been able to consistently produce high levels of achievement among students. An easy way to jump-start a collection of best practices is to meet with these people and interview them:

- What did you do differently from others to get these results?
- How do you know?

Be sure to record their information, using some type of collection instrument. Figure 12.2 provides a sample form that can be used to capture the essential tacit information that people think made the difference. Other sources of best practices include:

Students: Most students can identify their favorite lesson or unit that got them excited about learning. Giving them time to talk about their experiences can reveal practices worthy of investigation. I remember students asking me to visit a history teacher, who designed a unit on the Battle of Gettysburg to teach the Civil War. He transformed his classroom into an exciting learning center with artifacts, stories, and numerous opportunities for students to engage in work that was rigorous, yet fun. His techniques in student engagement were valuable pieces of tacit information that needed to be transferred to colleagues, throughout the school.

Teachers: Many teachers can identify their best lesson, curriculum unit, or classroom assessment. They just need some prodding to share them with colleagues. Principals can invent ways to collect best practices and provide recognition to their teachers, by using a little creativity. For example, consider asking each teacher to submit their best work, so that it can be placed into a formally bound "staff journal" that will be distributed to everyone on the faculty. Done the right way, it can turn into an annual tradition that enables people to take pride in their work and get accolades from fellow teachers.

Special Education Staff: Special education teachers and aides are in teacher's classrooms all of the time. In many cases, they probably know more about the strengths and weaknesses of the school's curriculum, instruction, and assessment than the principal. Their success in meeting the needs of mainstreamed students requires close examination of classroom experiences. They are excellent sources of where to find best practices.

Encouraging Knowledge Transfer

Encouraging people to share best practices will be challenging for several reasons. First, teachers are sensitive adults and don't want to give their colleagues

Figure 12.2. Best Practice Collection Form

Best Practices

Source: _____

Name/s

_____

Grade level/subjects

☐ Curriculum
☐ Assessment   (Check all appropriate boxes)
☐ Instruction

Description of Successful Practice:

_____

_____

_____

_____

_____

_____

_____

_____

_____

Results of Successful Practice:

_____

_____

_____

_____

_____

_____

_____

_____

_____

Please attach copies of any artifacts that were used in the best practice.

the impression that their techniques are superior to others. Second, with increased level of accountability for results on state assessments, some teachers believe that if they give away their best plans, others will rise to their level of performance. Sounds funny, but this is an unfortunate reality in many schools. Third, there is a prevailing belief that if teachers created something without the help of others, it becomes part of their unique persona, and defines their classroom in way that sets them apart from others. Some don't want to give this up.

All of these issues are symptomatic of a school culture that is entrenched in isolated work. Your challenge will be to shift the culture to one that seeks knowledge and shares it. Effective principals have found it useful to attack this problem by coming at it in a different way. In order to encourage the transfer of best practices, they provide mechanisms for teachers to ask one another for good ideas within the context of something that is timely in the classroom. Figure 12.3 illustrates a sample request form that teachers can send out to solicit help from each other. This is an effective way of encouraging transfer of best practices that softens many of the issues of sharing.

With adequate time to reflect on this, you will come up with other ideas on how to encourage teachers to identify best practices that fit with the culture of your school. Also, think about some type of recognition and reward system for those who come forward. Personal notes and accolades can serve as positive reinforcements, as well as formal mentions of these acts in the teacher evaluation process.

Creating Knowledge Transfer

Jack Grayson (1998), one of the leading experts on knowledge transfer, encouraged leaders to create infrastructures that support the transfer of knowledge. He identified three general designs that are used in the private sector. And with some slight modifications, principals can utilize these to create successful transfer within their schools:

1. Self-directed
2. Knowledge services and networks
3. Facilitated transfer

Self-directed infrastructures typically use some type of database that serves as a repository for best practices that can be deposited or accessed by individual users. Although this provides a good place to transfer knowledge, many schools don't have the resources to set up this type of system. It is also less personal and limited in encouraging people to invest their time in both contributing and accessing. For larger schools that do have the capability to create a database, it can provide a means of collecting best practices that is systematic and searchable. For other schools, using the documents shared in Figures 12.2 and 12.3 will be sufficient, as long as someone sets up some type of electronic or

---

Figure 12.3. Encouraging Transfer—Help Request

NEED YOUR IDEAS

Sender: _____
(Name)

Hi, I'm working on:
☐ Curriculum
☐ Assessment
☐ Instruction

_____
_____
_____
_____
_____
_____
_____
_____

and need your help. Do you have any ideas that I could use to:
(specify result)

_____
_____
_____

hard copy file that allow teachers to contribute and access the information with relative ease.

Knowledge Networks bring people together to learn each other's practices in a face-to-face setting that is more natural and conducive to sharing tacit knowledge that sometimes is hard to describe in writing. Principals can set up an infrastructure that enables teams and departments to have adequate time that promotes the sharing of quality curriculum, assessment, and instructional practices across grade levels and departments. Before scheduling in-service days, with one-size-fits-all training, think about providing teachers with a means of transferring best practices that already reside within the school. It also makes sense to look at the teacher workday and calendar to arrange multiple opportunities for teachers to share best practices. If your school has already implemented professional learning communities you are part way there, and will need to visit their meetings to discuss how best practices can be a regular part of their agenda.

Facilitated Transfer is perhaps the most direct and effective means of transfer by which identified people in the organization take the initiative to capture best practices and help staff implement them in the work setting. It goes beyond capturing and distributing best practice knowledge and information by creating transfer that coaches the recipient through the deployment of a best practice. Implementing this type of transfer in the school setting involves teacher leaders and volunteers, who have the expertise to not only share the practice, but work directly with a teacher or group of teachers to ensure that it is replicated correctly. This process will require the principal to make changes in staff assignments, but with careful planning, can create a powerful means of knowledge transfer that drives best practices deep into the daily work of the school. Some schools have hired substitutes as an initial means of supporting this process, while others have created partial day assignments for lead teachers to observe and replicate best practices. Before setting this type of infrastructure in place, principals will need to plan and collaborate with teachers on the best strategies that will accomplish facilitated transfer in their particular school setting.

Completing Knowledge Transfer

Let's assume that you have set into place a variety of support mechanisms to ensure that best practices have been shared with teachers throughout the school. How do you make sure that people are really participating in the transfers? This will depend on the primary vehicles you have introduced. If you put a self-directed system in place, you will want to check on the volume of exchanges, as well as the quality of the knowledge deposited. If you have a data base, you will need to monitor the flow of information that moves in and out as well as the content. Consider assigning a master teacher to perform this work so that some type of quality control process is maintained.

Knowledge networks can be monitored by visiting and observing the meetings where best practices are exchanged. You can also ask someone on the team to submit a follow-up report, or copy of minutes, that document the completed transfer of a best practice. Figure 12.4 illustrates a request form that can be used to document the knowledge that was transferred as a result of knowledge network transfer. The form combines a request to network as well as a commitment to document the results.

Facilitated transfers are the easiest to monitor because specific people within the organization are assigned to facilitate and deliver the transfer. Under this type of infrastructure, the principal can request monthly reports and meetings to review the progress of completed transfers of best practices throughout the school.

Evaluating Transfer

Experts in the field of knowledge management (O'Dell & Grayson) stress the importance of evaluating the impact of each endeavor to share best practices. The ultimate purpose of knowledge transfer is to get better results. The most concrete evidence in a school is higher performance levels on state assessments, standardized tests, and formative assessments. How to track this in a manner that is least cumbersome will be the challenge. A practical approach is to handle this by threading the documented results to the paper trail of knowledge transfers that were put into place. Figure 12.5 displays one means of evaluating the transfer of a best practice by attaching evidence of the completed work. In simple terms, we want to know if the transferred practice yielded similar success for the user. Did the teacher or team of teachers successfully replicate the best practice so that the results turned out the same way?

It is important to attach and file the results of the successful transfer for another reason. In many cases, the user of the transfer finds ways to improve on the best practice so that it yields even higher results. Capturing those improvements will be critical to future users.

Assuring Knowledge is Used and Improved

Talk to any lab researcher and they will tell you that they are careful to document any modifications made in an experiment. They never know when they will intentionally or accidentally cause a better result. The same is true of teachers who use each other's best practices and discover improvements that yield an even better result than the original provider was able to produce.

Figure 12.5 includes a section to capture two essential parts to a new and improved discovery when implementing a best practice. First, it allows the implementer(s) a means of sharing their improvements with the originator(s).

Figure 12.4. Requesting/Documenting Completion of Knowledge Transfer

KNOWLEDGE TRANSFER REQUEST

Knowledge and/or Skills to be Transferred:

_____

_____

_____

_____

_____

RECIPIENT(S)   _____

_____

_____

_____

_____

PROVIDER(S)   ☐ Mentoring
☐ Shadowing
☐ Vertical Team to Vertical Team
☐ Grade Level to Grade Level
☐ Department to Department
☐ Vertical Team to Grade Level
☐ Grade Level to Vertical Team
☐ Other (Explain) _____

GOAL: _____

_____

_____

_____

Date(s): _____   Time(s): _____

Evidence of Knowledge Transfer:

_____

_____

_____

_____

_____

Figure 12.5. Knowledge Transfer Follow-Up

EVALUATING/IMPROVING KNOWLEDGE TRANSFER
FOLLOW-UP REPORT

Knowledge transferred:

_____
_____
_____
_____
_____

How is the knowledge being used?

_____
_____
_____
_____
_____

How could the transfer be more effective in the future?

_____
_____
_____
_____
_____

How have you improved on the knowledge that was transferred?

_____
_____
_____
_____
_____

Provider Signature: _____ Date: _____
Provider Signature: _____ Date: _____
Provider Signature: _____ Date: _____
Recipient Signature: _____ Date: _____
Recipient Signature: _____ Date: _____
Recipient Signature: _____ Date: _____

Second, it provides a mechanism that sends the improvement back through the knowledge transfer process (see Figure 12.1).

Finally, the assurance that knowledge transfers are being used and improved does not have to fall on the shoulders of the principal. Rather, it is the responsibility of the principal to ensure that a system is set into place that facilitates this last, and most important step in the knowledge transfer process.

Improving Curriculum, Assessment, and Instruction

Why not just import improvements to curriculum, assessment, and instruction? You can, but remember that teachers have been overwhelmed with mandated programs from outside the school and resist artificial implants to their classrooms. Central offices have attempted to standardize curriculum guides, lesson plans, and formative assessments as though there is trust in the people they have hired to deliver quality learning. They fail to understand that each campus has its own unique culture and evolutionary stage in the change process. To think that a uniform road map will cause districtwide improvement is a futile exercise.

Each Campus is Different

It has been my experience that the variability in the quality of curriculum, assessment, and instruction is considerable, from one school campus to the next, even when they belong to the same school district. For this reason, students are the recipients of educational experiences that differ quite a bit from school to school. The principal's role in this inequity is to engage the faculty in the identification of existing challenges and develop strategies that transfer data and best practices across the faculty.

Using Data to Improve Curriculum, Assessment, and Instruction

Too often, data is overlooked and principals miss the opportunity to shape a new vision for a school around the notion of taking what we know and sharing new ideas and solutions. But in the case of Velasquez Elementary in suburban Houston, Beth Dow used data to inspire her staff to create a campus where every student would experience success (Berkey & Dow, 2008). By examining past practices that were common to school cultures, the staff created new processes and practices that threaded improvements to curriculum, assessment, and instruction throughout the campus. Through collaborative meetings and discussions, teachers and administrators mapped out the following plan:

Old Practice	New Practice
Use of minimum state standards to monitor learning	☐ Development of campus standards at higher levels of Bloom's Taxonomy
School success measured by state assessments	☐ Student success monitored by weekly common formative assessments
Student progress measured and held by individual teacher	☐ Student progress measured and shared by teams of teachers and administrators
Remedial work determined and delivered by individual teacher	☐ Corrective instruction designed and delivered by team of teachers, specialists, and administrators
One pace for all student learning	☐ Pace is adjusted per learner

Dow organized her staff into multiple teams so that modifications to curriculum, assessment, and instruction flowed both horizontally and vertically among teams of teachers. As principal, she led a team of administrators, specialists, and master teachers in creating a "war room," where data was posted, analyzed, and used to drive weekly strategy meetings to address students and teachers needing support. The school culture became one where successful practices were not only identified, but shared and replicated across all teams throughout the school. In their first year of transformation, the school earned the highest distinction from the Texas Education Agency.

What Great Principals Do

In their book, *First Break All the Rules*, Buckingham & Coffman (1999) revealed what the world's best managers do. They interviewed hundreds of successful managers of over 400 companies and found that, in spite of varying sexes, races, and ages, they all shared a common characteristic: They begin by breaking the conventional wisdom that keeps organizations trapped. As I reflect on my career and exceptional opportunities to work and collaborate with great school leaders, it is apparent that they too broke the rules to improve their schools. As we have discussed, teachers have the greatest impact on student achievement once children set foot on their campuses. We also know that curriculum, assessment, and instruction are the key ingredients that will determine the quality of the educational experiences and successes of our students. Thus, it makes sense that great principals find ways to engage their faculty in constant improvements to those ingredients, regardless of the state, central office, and past practices. Great principals take risks and move the culture of the school outside the box of conventional wisdom, and when teachers make gains, the leader ensures that all of the relevant information on how the progress was achieved is shared and replicated throughout the campus.

The lasting changes that schools can achieve depend on the principal's ability to provide a level of autonomy, encouragement, and support to teachers. With a reconstituted vision directed on individual and collaborative efforts to improve curriculum, assessment, and instruction, teachers can accomplish great things by tapping the internal talent and best practices of each other.

Principals must not only facilitate these conditions and processes, but also remain current in their personal knowledge of best practices throughout the profession. When teachers need help, the principal cannot simply hand them a book or send them to a workshop. Principals must engage in thoughtful discussions that demonstrate a working knowledge of current best practices in the profession and a clear awareness of the talent within the school that can be tapped. Here are just a few of the expectations that principals are using in their collaborative work with teachers:

Curriculum

✓ Standards that add greater definition to state and local curriculum
✓ Supplements to curriculum that challenge students beyond mastery
✓ Skills and knowledge associated with workforce readiness

Assessment

✓ Assessments that drill down to daily and weekly mastery of objectives
✓ Assessments that provide specific feedback for immediate intervention
✓ Assessments that include significant stretch beyond minimum standards

Instruction

✓ Instruction that is differentiated and ensures mastery for each child
✓ Instruction that is engaging at a level comparable to competing interests of children
✓ Instruction that inspires learners and provides meaning within the context of their daily lives.

Tracker Goals for Your Consideration: Engaging Staff in Knowledge Transfer

Knowledge Transfer:

I will . . .
1. Design a process to identify best practices in curriculum, assessment, and instruction in the school.
2. Encourage the transfer of best practices among teachers.
3. Create the means for transfer of best practices within the school.
4. Ensure the completion of best practice transfers within the school.
5. Evaluate the transfer of best practices within the school.
6. Assure that best practices are used and improved in the school.

Improving Curriculum, Assessment, and Instruction:

I will . . .

1. Protect teachers from mandated changes and work with them to utilize best practices within the school to improve curriculum, assessment, and instruction.
2. Keep myself informed of current best practices in the field.
3. Engage teachers in an audit of the curriculum to ensure high standards and quality learning.
4. Facilitate the preparation of quality assessments that inform teachers and diagnose learning problems.
5. Provide teachers with adequate time to collaborate on improvements to curriculum, assessment, and instruction.

Chapter 13

Observing and Coaching the Learning Process

He has the right to criticize who has the heart to help.

—ABRAHAM LINCOLN

The most important duty of a principal is to ensure that each child receives a quality education. This requires principals to invest a majority of their time visiting classrooms, monitoring instruction, providing feedback and support to teachers, resolving learning problems, and creating networks among professionals to maximize academic growth for each child. In this chapter we will examine the most critical piece of the Effective Principal Tracker and offer strategies that will improve your engagement of teachers in reaching the vision of the school in every classroom. Using the fundamental concepts of instructional leadership, we will build a rhythm of practices that blend the role of the principal as teacher and learner, so that the two become one and your relationship with teachers centers on a shared commitment to improved learning for every child.

Focused Classroom Walk-throughs

Much has been written about the use of classroom walk-throughs to improve instruction, and like many educational initiatives, application of this strategy has ranged from weak to strong. Some schools have simply repackaged their teacher evaluation process by handing principals a traditional checklist and sending them into classrooms for shorter periods of time. Other schools have done a magnificent job of implementing walk-throughs as a supportive process in which principals serve as coaches, mentors, co-teachers, and facilitators. Some of the discrepancies are due to central office control, while others can be attributed to the comfort level and skills of the principal. For this reason, walk-throughs must be preceded with an identified purpose.

Following the Vision

Ask teachers about the last time that a formal observation process changed their behaviors in the classroom and they will smile and politely tell you that it was just a process to comply with district expectations. In most cases, once the procedures were completed and the paperwork signed and filed, the principal's visits to the classroom ended for the school year. The purpose of the endeavor was to comply with policy, and as long as the principal and teacher fulfilled their obligations, everyone, including central office, was satisfied. Effective principals recognize this dilemma and incorporate a parallel process that reintroduces the purpose of classroom visits as a means of developing collegial relationships with teachers and collaborative efforts to improve the quality of learning for each child.

The purpose of our approach to walk-throughs will be quite clear. Using a vision that is shaped around common expectations of curriculum, assessment, and instruction, the principal and teacher use the classroom as a lab to improve each of these elements. Judgment is suspended in favor of learning and growing together. Instruction moves away from teaching to a test and toward an ongoing set of experiments to ratchet up the effectiveness of the learning experiences for each child. The work of the principal and teacher becomes purpose driven, instead of policy mandated. The relationship between the principal and the staff is built on trust and doing whatever is required to succeed.

Before embarking on the use of classroom walk-throughs, it will be important to hold discussions with the faculty to discuss purpose, expectations, and the processes to be incorporated, so that people understand your intentions. A practical approach to the implementation is to set up the first visits as a pilot exercise, so that everyone can get comfortable with the notion that they will be an equal partner in the experience. Start with a review of the vision that was created and the expectations that the school has committed to fulfilling. Using the example of the vision from chapter 10, let's examine some talking points that a principal could use, in an exchange with the faculty:

As we practice the walk-throughs, what is a reasonable approach to:

♦ Knowing the learning objective of the lesson
♦ Recognizing the context of the activities of the lesson
♦ Understanding the relationship between curriculum, instruction, and assessment in the lesson
♦ Exchanging feedback about the lesson

Be prepared for a considerable amount of discourse as teachers question the issue of trust in the context of their past experiences with evaluation systems that left them feeling like players in a game. Give them time to vent, question, and push back. Trust takes time, and moving the culture towards an open and collegial arena requires patience and understanding. If you provide a forum to establish initial expectations for walk-throughs, a majority of teachers will offer suggestions like the following:

- The principal will enter the classroom in a way that is least disruptive
- The teacher will continue the lesson, but will also feel free to invite the principal to participate as appropriate
- The focus of the first walk-through will be a snapshot of the relation between the learning objective, the lesson, and the assessment of students
- The teacher and principal will exchange a handwritten copy of a triangle containing their perception of the alignment of curriculum, instruction, and assessment that were present during the time of the walk-through
- The teacher and principal will meet informally for ten minutes, sometime after the walk-through, to debrief and compare notes

Whatever is agreed upon, make sure that you adhere to the expectations during the walk-throughs. Spend a considerable amount of time talking to the faculty as you proceed, so that rumors, issues, and misconceptions can be addressed. Trust building is the first and most important step. It also is wise to hold meetings with departments and grade levels to get feedback on how the process is working, and make necessary adjustments.

As teachers become comfortable with the process, they will eventually want more feedback that gives them a sense of your interest in their classrooms. This is a signal that the culture is beginning to shift, and you are ready to broaden the purpose of the walk-through experience and get deeper into the vision of the school. Engaging the faculty in a big picture discussion of what was learned in the pilot phase can set up a dialogue on how the walk-through process can evolve into a shared learning experience for both the principal and the teacher. The goal is to reach consensus on the next steps to practice in making the experience worthwhile and meaningful in the pursuit of the vision of the school. Figure 13.1 and 13.2 display sample forms that were designed, using the common vision of a school and completed by the principal during a walk-through.

Figure 13.3 displays the principal's version of the form. In this school, the principal and staff agreed that the new procedure would be as follows:

Step 1—Principal does walk-through and leaves feedback on the desk of the teacher using the new form

Step 2—Teacher completes a second walk-through form that reflects his/her input on what transpired during the visit

Step 3—Teacher and principal meet to debrief and share what each learned

Figure 13.4 displays the teacher's version of the completed walk-through form. Notice that in some cases, both checked and commented on the same elements of the vision, while in others, they came up with additional feedback

Figure 13.1. Sample Walk-Through Form—Principal's Version

☑ **Observer**
☐ **Teacher**

Instruction
☐ _____
☐ _____
☐ _____

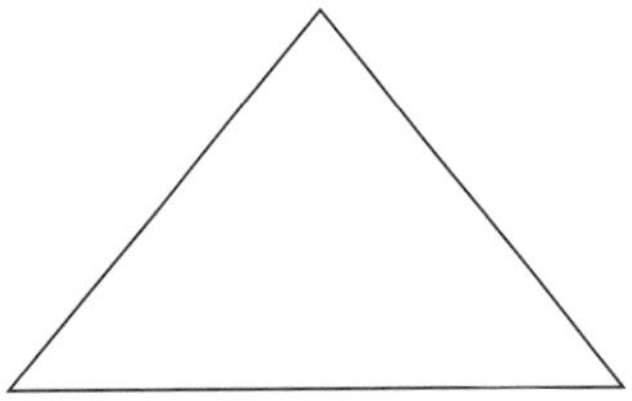

Curriculum
☐ _____
☐ _____
☐ _____

Assessment
☐ _____
☐ _____
☐ _____

Instruction: _____

Curriculum: _____

Assessment: _____

Figure 13.2. Sample Walk-Through Form—Teacher's Version

☐ **Observer**
☑ **Teacher**

Instruction
☐ _____
☐ _____
☐ _____

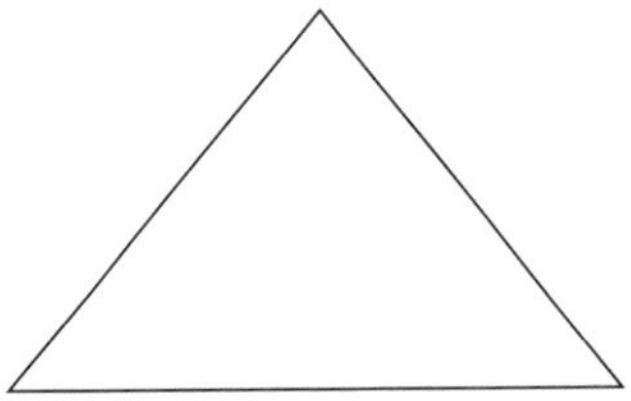

Curriculum
☐ _____
☐ _____
☐ _____

Assessment
☐ _____
☐ _____
☐ _____

Instruction: _____

Curriculum: _____

Assessment: _____

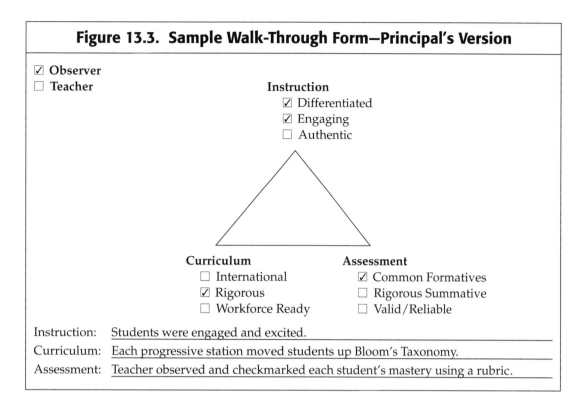

Figure 13.3. Sample Walk-Through Form—Principal's Version

☑ Observer
☐ Teacher

Instruction
    ☑ Differentiated
    ☑ Engaging
    ☐ Authentic

Curriculum
    ☐ International
    ☑ Rigorous
    ☐ Workforce Ready

Assessment
    ☑ Common Formatives
    ☐ Rigorous Summative
    ☐ Valid/Reliable

Instruction: Students were engaged and excited.

Curriculum: Each progressive station moved students up Bloom's Taxonomy.

Assessment: Teacher observed and checkmarked each student's mastery using a rubric.

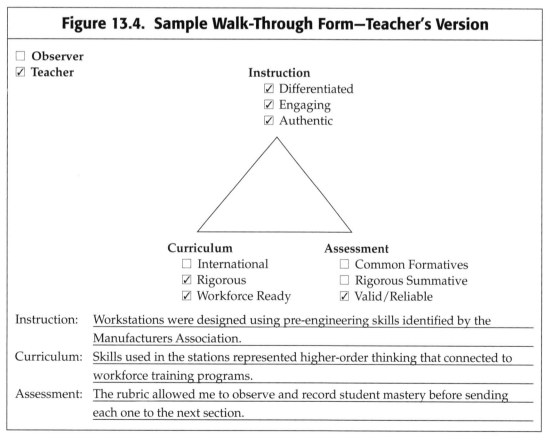

Figure 13.4. Sample Walk-Through Form—Teacher's Version

☐ Observer
☑ Teacher

Instruction
    ☑ Differentiated
    ☑ Engaging
    ☑ Authentic

Curriculum
    ☐ International
    ☑ Rigorous
    ☑ Workforce Ready

Assessment
    ☐ Common Formatives
    ☐ Rigorous Summative
    ☑ Valid/Reliable

Instruction: Workstations were designed using pre-engineering skills identified by the Manufacturers Association.

Curriculum: Skills used in the stations represented higher-order thinking that connected to workforce training programs.

Assessment: The rubric allowed me to observe and record student mastery before sending each one to the next section.

that was different. This approach has several benefits. First, it maintains a walk-through process that is highly focused on the vision of the school. Second, it provides both the observer and the teacher with an opportunity to share impressions and follow up with a conversation. Third, it creates a relationship whereby both parties are teachers as well as learners.

We haven't discussed the length of walk-throughs, and this is a potential issue, particularly if the experience becomes rigid. Many of the writers and researchers in the practice of walk-throughs suggest times ranging from 3–15 minutes (Downey). It makes sense to collaborate with the faculty on this issue, but also allow for flexibility on whatever is agreed upon. The principal needs to be in the classroom long enough to capture a snapshot of the lesson, without turning the experience into a visit that resembles a formal observation. It also is important to recognize that walk-throughs must be natural, unannounced, and free of stress. If you walk into a classroom that for some reason does not lend itself to a visit, simply walk away. Sometimes the students are involved in assessments or activities that cannot be disrupted, so be understanding and build trust by respecting the needs of the teacher.

Ultimately, the walk-through experience should continue to evolve to a point where the principal can take a more active role in coaching, mentoring, and experimenting with teachers in a manner that develops strong partnerships and trusting relationships that help each classroom get closer to the vision. In order to accomplish this, principals will need to incorporate some of the basic skills and techniques associated with coaching.

Coaching Effective Teaching

There are a variety of coaching models and programs that principals can introduce in the school setting. Some focus on basic classroom management, while others are specific to instructional improvement in content areas such as reading. Our work will be centered on the principal's role in coaching for the following purposes:

- To provide feedback and support in the classroom walk-through process
- To train effective teachers in coaching their colleagues
- To lead teachers in reaching the vision of the school

Taking a Cue from Effective Coaches

Great coaches share a number of characteristics that contribute to their effectiveness. They know their craft and communicate techniques and processes that improve the performance of each player. They are good observers and listeners and seek to make incremental improvements in the performance of each person. Effective coaches praise the gains people make, and give specific feedback that is helpful, but not demeaning. They also recognize that each person has varying skill levels, as well as personality, motivation, and drive that can be taken into consideration when customizing interactions.

Providing Feedback

As you begin the walk-through process, it will be important to practice the skill of giving feedback in a manner and style that is helpful to teachers and respectful of their work. You are seeing a snapshot of the classroom, and therefore the information you collect on a feedback form and share in a face-to-face meeting will have limits. The best way to approach a collegial exchange is to first be a good listener and seek to understand the information that the teacher is sharing. By casting yourself first as a learner, you open the door to ask questions that clarify and give context to the setting you observed. Here are some of the tips that leaders in the field of supervision and coaching have identified when providing feedback (Zepeda, 2003; Danielson & McGreal, 2000; Gottesman, 2000):

✓ Use language that is neutral and nonjudgmental
✓ Ask questions that seek to clarify, not intimidate
✓ Provide factual information on what you observed and allow for corrections

Remember that the walk-through is not an evaluation of the teacher, but an opportunity for you to observe the quality of learning experiences as they relate to the vision of the school. Not all walk-throughs will be followed with a meeting. Sometimes the dialogue can take place after several visits and an accumulation of feedback forms.

Differentiated Coaching

People have varying learning styles and personality types and thus experts in the field of professional coaching suggest that it makes sense to differentiate strategies when working with teachers (Kise, 2006). Many schools have put their staff through Myers-Briggs training and other types of assessments that offer good information on how and why we behave and react to each other in different ways. Effective coaches understand this and take the unique qualities of adults into consideration when coaching.

Coaching can also be differentiated by the level of skills and knowledge of the individual. For example, as you become more familiar with the strengths and weaknesses of teachers, in relationship to their effectiveness in delivering curriculum, assessment, and instruction, it enables you to see the opportunities for growth and improvement in each person. This will also become invaluable to you when the campus is ready for peer coaching.

Peer Coaching

In the previous chapter we discussed the value of transferring critical knowledge from one part of an organization to another. One of the most effective means of accomplishing this in the school setting is to train highly effective teachers in the fundamentals of coaching and create a network of people who can support the professional growth of the staff. Through a collaborative process, the principal can work with teachers to design a process that frees up master teachers who are willing to utilize their expertise in collaborating with colleagues to improve each classroom. This is not limited to instruction. A school needs coaches who can help teachers with modifications and enhancements to the curriculum and instruction, as well as improvements to formative and summative assessments. Other forms of peer coaching include the acclimation of new teachers into the culture and expectations of the school. Some schools have handpicked effective teachers to serve as instructional coaches to a cadre of new teachers, in order to help them get comfortable with the vision of the school and the expectations for the classroom.

Resolving Learning Problems

As the school drives the vision deeper into each classroom and the principal and staff see children who are struggling, it is a great opportunity to step back and think about a process that engages everyone in addressing learning problems. Many schools experience issues associated with children at the bottom as well as the top of each class. Effective principals raise the question of how the culture of the school will ensure that the needs of these children are addressed in a timely and effective manner. Too often, schools wait until a progress report or grade card delivers the news of poor performance, and both the child and the parent are left searching for answers. One of the most important jobs of an effective principal is to work with teachers in the design of a system that captures the information that a child is struggling and react immediately to resolve the problem.

Networking

When a child experiences a learning difficulty, it is the shared responsibility of all professionals to work together, much in the same way that a hospital responds in an emergency room. Those patients who are in a life-threatening state get priority attention, and others are eventually treated as soon as the resources are available. Schools must take the same approach by sharing critical information, developing strategies, and assigning duties to specialists to remedy the problem. Here are some common steps that a principal should include when designing a collaborative network to help kids who are experiencing learning problems:

Step 1. Get an effective data system in place to measure daily and weekly performance of each child. Data is critical in the identification process, and many schools have developed common formative assessments to monitor mastery of objectives on a regular basis. If your school does not have these types of assessments in place, you will need to rely on individual teachers to identify children who are struggling with the assignments and work in the classroom.

Step 2. Design a communication system that captures the name and specific learning problem of any student who continues to struggle after the teacher has exhausted multiple strategies to resolve the issue.

Step 3. Create a team of professionals who can come together on a regular basis to review the emergency list of students needing additional help and formulate strategies to correct the problem. The principal should be actively involved in leading or overseeing the meetings so that the necessary resources are deployed and that swift action is taken.

Step 4. Assign members of the team to visit classrooms and provide teaching and interventions to help children get back on track.

Step 5. Review the results of the intervention with the team and design new strategies for any student who continues to struggle.

You probably are wondering about staffing. Where do you find people to serve on such a team? Focusing the roles of people such as guidance counselors, deans, assistant principals, specialists, and aides on providing emergency services becomes the first priority of their workday. Your leadership will be essential in not only leading the team, but also modeling the importance of reaching each child and ensuring success.

Reaching all Learners

Dr. William Sanders (1997) accumulated one of the largest longitudinal data bases of student achievement in the U.S., and through the development of a value-added model, has provided schools with valuable insights into the impact of teachers on the annual academic growth of children. Through multiple studies, he has been able to demonstrate that the variability of effectiveness from one teacher to another accounts for the greatest discrepancies we see in the achievement of students. Some teachers are highly effective with children at the bottom of a class and less effective with those at the top. Others teach to the middle and provide little growth for children at both ends of the spectrum.

Effective principals observe the learning processes that are used throughout the school and serve as a safeguard to some of the ineffective practices that hold children back. Some of these include the following:

♦ Assigning enrichment work to advanced learners instead of accelerating them

- Assigning special education students to basic classes or pullouts that are not associated with their identified learning disability
- Tracking students into low-level courses based on their behavior issues
- Allowing teacher generalists to alter learning time in subjects such as mathematics based on preference instead of student needs
- Wasting learning time at the beginning and ending of class
- Asking advanced learners to help other students until the class catches up
- Using computer time as a reward instead of an expectation for all
- Lowering expectations for mastery among students who need more time
- Using the first six weeks of school to review the previous year's curriculum
- Intimidating learners with unreasonable expectations so that they drop the class
- Assigning busywork and showing videos on Friday afternoons
- Relying on true/false, multiple choice assessments instead of higher order assessments that take longer to grade

I share these not to demean the wonderful and dedicated teachers who put forth their best every day, but to alert principals to some of the habits and ineffective practices that do academic harm to children. I have witnessed all of the above at various times in my career and underscore the point that it is the obligation of the principal to not only monitor weak practices, but have the courage to address them.

Finally, throughout this chapter we have emphasized the importance of getting into classrooms and working collaboratively with teachers to improve learning for all children. The work of the principal in leading these efforts is critical to bringing clarity to expectations, moving people toward the vision, and deepening relationships that are bound by an unwavering commitment to children. In the next chapter we will look at ways to keep your leadership skills sharp and out in front of the people who depend on you for guidance and support.

Tracker Goals for Your Consideration: Observing and Coaching the Learning Process

Focused Classroom Walk-Throughs:

I will . . .

1. Work with teachers to design a walk-through process that engages teachers in a shared examination of their daily efforts to reach the vision of the school.
2. Seek feedback from teachers about their walk-through experiences.

Coaching Effective Teaching:

I will . . .

1. Provide teachers with effective coaching that is differentiated and based on their individual needs in the improvement of curriculum, assessment, and instruction.
2. Design a training program for master teachers to acquire coaching skills for the purpose of helping fellow teachers improve their performance.

Resolving Learning Problems:

I will . . .

1. Design a system to identify and rectify learning problems of children through the engagement of staff in intervention processes and corrective instruction.
2. Engage teachers in shared learning and transfer of best practices to improve the learning process of each student.

Reaching All Learners:

I will . . .

1. Monitor the learning of all children and confront practices that inhibit or hurt their academic progress.
2. Create learning networks that share information on each student and generate solutions to learning problems.

Chapter 14

Expanding Knowledge and Skills

A man can learn only two ways, one by reading, and the other by association with smarter people.

—WILL ROGERS

Rogers's quote reveals a great strategy for leaders who find themselves short on time, especially when it comes to reading and staying up with new developments in their field. Principals face the same challenge and often resort to attendance at state and national conventions as an opportunity to catch their breath and reflect on things they should be doing. But there are a good number of other sources of professional growth that can be embedded into the work setting. In this chapter we will help you explore a variety of strategies to keep your leadership skills sharp and aligned to the vision of the school. Change has been a consistent theme throughout this book and principals must invest in their own staff development in order to model their personal commitment to behaving as both a learner and a teacher.

Sharing and Learning with Other Leaders

No one likes to go it alone when changing their behaviors. The person going on a diet or breaking a habit such as smoking is always encouraged by experts to find a partner and a support system to share and learn from each other. In chapter 3, we developed an internal support system to help you with the changes that occur as you reduce daily time in areas that are traditional and unproductive in reaching the vision of the school. But other than central office administrators, we didn't include other leaders who can be great partners in your transformation as well as professional growth. For this reason, current additions to pre-service training for principals include methods of networking with other leaders to share and practice together (Berkey & Hutto, 2008).

Other Principals

Principals have few opportunities to network with colleagues, especially those outside of the district in which they work. In my own experiences, I found it refreshing to have the chance to speak to other principals at a conference or in a monthly meeting of the athletic league. Many times, our conversations involved trouble shooting similar issues, sharing new ideas, and commiserating about the overloaded menu of responsibilities heaped upon our desks. All of these topics point to an untapped source to expand your knowledge and skills while going through changes in your school and your leadership.

As you prepare to implement the models introduced in this book, think about soliciting a principal or cadre of principals from other schools to take on the challenge together. It won't be difficult finding principals who are facing the same challenges and want to get control of their daily workload, and more importantly, scale up the academic performance of their students. The first challenge is to get commitment, and the obvious barrier will be time. But if you put your minds together, you can come up with strategies that will enable you to create your own learning community and provide access to each other on a regular basis. With some innovative techniques, you can set times to meet face-to-face as well as online and over the phone, so that learning is timely, yet respectful of busy schedules. Setting parameters will also make it easier for colleagues to commit, so begin with an understanding that no one will miss critical time from their school day when children are in session. Here are a few strategies that principals have used to create effective networks among themselves:

Monthly Dinner Meetings: Provide a social setting that allows principals to build their relationships and discuss progress with the changes they are implementing. Sometimes it is easy to schedule these around shared athletic events or common meetings such as state or locally sponsored workshops.

E-mail Distribution Lists: Give the opportunity to carry on asynchronous discussions that facilitate an exchange of problems, strategies, and, sometimes, a need to simply vent. It will be important to set some type of reasonable expectation that members respond within a day or two, whatever meets the comfort level of the group.

Cell Phone Hotline: Allow the members to have the security of knowing they can call each other whenever they are in the middle of a problem and need a colleague to talk them through a situation. Sometimes it takes a calm and rational friend you can trust to help you through a decision or crisis.

Shared Conferences: Enable the group to learn together at a conference that connects with a shared issue among their schools. It also provides quality time to review each other's progress and exchange successes and challenges.

All Calls: Permit a principal who is faced with an emergency or critical problem to call the group together on short notice. This requires a commitment from the other members to respond and should be limited to those situations in which a colleague cannot use the other modes of communication to resolve the issue.

Creating a successful learning community among other principals will require that everyone sees themselves as a learner and that there is nothing wrong with asking for help. Too often we believe that doing so is a sign of weakness rather than one of confidence and strength. Having some initial discussions about norms for the group such as checking egos at the door, or "What's said in Vegas, stays in Vegas," will be important to build trust and strong relationships.

Retired Administrators

Every community has retired administrators and seeking out these people has a lot of promise for support and friendship as you transform your practices. In fact, some of the leading projects in school leadership transformation throughout the country utilize retired school principals in their delivery models. They can be used in a variety of ways to help you implement changes in your leadership practices and initiatives. Some principals have used them to "substitute" by picking up some of the traditional duties while they spend their days working with teachers. Others have found retired principals with instructional leadership experience who can coach them in effective practices. They can also serve as observers and evaluators of your work so that you get a close set of eyes on your progress. In other situations, retired principals have been used as another set of hands in important work with teachers to write curriculum, develop formative assessments, and implement new instructional strategies. Finding retirees with the right skill sets is important, and a good source for locating them is your state and local principal associations. Many retired administrators maintain their membership and affiliation with their state associations, and therefore can be just a few phone calls away. Many of them find it is a wonderful experience and will be willing to do this on a voluntary basis. Some districts have been supportive with special stipends or supplemental contracts to provide compensation. Private and public grants have also been used to support this resource.

State Associations

State associations are very responsive to the needs of their members and offer a variety of services that you can tap. Many of them have a hotline that is available for questions, advice, and support. Professional development is one of their main concerns and talking to them about your interests and needs is a smart thing to do. Principal associations have a vast network of resources for principals, and you will find that they are responsive to requests and anxious to lend support. If you develop your own learning community of fellow principals, consider using your association as a potential partner to customize training and identify best practices around the state that the group can access.

Local Leadership

Community and local business leadership face similar challenges and accessing them can bring you great benefits. I always made a point of meeting with the local mayor, law and safety chiefs, and juvenile court judges to learn from their leadership experiences of the community and establish a network of support. They represent a rich source of information and can advise you on the culture and issues that need to be navigated, as you make changes in the school. They are also familiar with many of the challenges that are common to leadership and can share their own strategies that have contributed to their success.

Local business leaders are another good source of leadership talent and expertise that few principals take into consideration. First, they are driven by results and can provide you with the skills and practices that have made them successful. Too often we see them as profiteers without respecting the strength and leadership that they have demonstrated in getting their people to focus on a vision and continuously improve results.

University Resources

Universities are always looking for partnerships, especially if they include an opportunity to conduct research. Professors are under the gun to publish, and keeping that in mind, consider contacting a local department of school leadership or business management that most likely will have a member looking to conduct a study. By offering yourself as the subject of a study in leadership transformation, you can provide an excellent opportunity to gain valuable leadership skills and free mentoring from an expert in the field. Don't worry about confidentiality because all studies of human subjects come under rules that will protect your identity.

Conducting Action Research

Action research provides a great opportunity to enhance your knowledge and skills through a project that focuses on a key area of the school's vision. It allows the principal to serve both as a learner and a teacher in a collaborative endeavor with staff in addressing a problem that, once resolved, will improve teaching and learning. Let's reflect on the previous example of a refined school vision that was shaped around the classroom and consider some potential action research problems that would be worthy of your consideration. Table 14.1 provides a list of questions that could serve as potential action research projects

Figure 14.1. Sample Action Research Problems				
Action Research Projects				
Vision Area	**Problem**	**Yes** ✓	**No** ✓	**Maybe** ✓
Curriculum: ■ International	How can we refine our curriculum so that it is competitive with other countries?			
■ Rigorous	How can we make our curriculum more rigorous?			
■ Workforce Ready	How can we ensure that our curriculum includes workforce readiness knowledge and skills?			
Assessment: ■ Common Formative	How can we develop common formatives that identify learning problems early enough to remedy?			
■ Rigorous Summatives	How can we integrate rigorous summatives that provide more stretch than the state assessments?			
■ Valid/Reliable	How can we revise our internal assessments so that they are more valid and reliable?			
Instruction: ■ Differentiated	How can we differentiate the process of instruction to meet the varying learning styles of each student?			
■ Engaging	How can we take existing lessons and make them more engaging?			
■ Authentic	How can we take existing lessons and make them more relevant to the lives or our students?			

that connect to curriculum, assessment, and instruction. All of these are appropriate questions that should be raised, given the vision of the school. By presenting these to the faculty, you can either arrive at consensus of which one to pursue, or modify the question so that it meets the needs of a more specific problem.

In work associated with the Brown University Northeast and Islands Regional Educational Laboratory (LAB), Eileen Ferrance (2000) offered the following steps to follow in an action research project:

Steps in Action Research

1. Identify the problem.
2. Gather data.
3. Interpret data.
4. Act on evidence.
5. Evaluate results.
6. Identify next steps.

Using the first problem identified in Figure 14.1, let's examine how a school could investigate international comparisons of school curricula and develop a project that would refine the schools standards, so that they are more competitive to what other children around the world are learning. Figure 14.2 displays sample steps that could be incorporated into the action research process, using LAB's model. In this example, the principal and staff decided to examine the curriculum of the Ministry of Singapore because their country consistently scores at the top of international comparisons in basic skill areas. The Ministry also make the curriculum available (in English) on their website, which made the gathering of data somewhat easy.

As you move through each step of an action research project, it will be important to use collaborative processes and consensus building so that teachers feel in control of the work and will be more likely to use the results to improve their classrooms. Principals can expand their knowledge of skills not only in the content of the project (in this case, international curriculum), but also practice coaching, collaborating, and building consensus around work that brings the campus vision to fruition.

Reading

Who has time to read? We all know the dilemma. After long hours and overflowing workloads, reading is considered a luxury to most principals. But without investing some quality time, you can get rusty and disconnected from the breadth and depth of important work in our field. I have found it useful to sort out the typical needs associated with professional reading and formulate some simple strategies to keep current.

Figure 14.2. Sample Action Research Plan

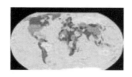

ACTION RESEARCH PROJECT
Vision Area: Curriculum
International

Problem identification:

Refining the curriculum so that it reflects international standards and enables children to acquire the same knowledge and skills that children in other countries are learning.

Gather data:

Download the subject curriculum from the Ministry of Singapore's website: www.moe.gov.sg

Interpret data:

Conduct a grade-level-by-grade-level comparison of our local curriculum with the equivalent grade level/subject curriculum of Singapore.

Action evidence:

Prepare draft revisions to the local curriculum, incorporating knowledge and skills from the Singapore curriculum.

Evaluate results:

Conduct an audit of the drafts to ensure coherence and vertical articulation.

Identify next steps:

Present curriculum for central office review and adoption. Use this project as a model for future work in integrating workforce readiness knowledge and skills into the curriculum.

Breadth of What's Going On: Perhaps the easiest way to stay on top of current developments is to use online sources and keep the list to a minimum. I suggest that you subscribe to some type of daily newspaper Listserv so that you remain connected to what is happening in the world. Remember, keeping the need for change issues in front of the staff will require that you keep finding sources.

The same holds true for professional news. *Education Week* is probably one of the best sources to keep you informed of state and national developments. They also offer a hard copy as well as online service and can place you on Listservs defined by your areas of need (curriculum, assessment, instruction, and leadership). Many of the profession journals offer similar services.

Depth of What's Going On: Books are plentiful, and our time to read them is limited. For this reason, it makes sense to first read some reviews before you invest your time. There are a variety of book review sections in most of the trade journals in education, and *Education Week* provides the same type of service. In keeping with the themes of this book, I suggest that ones on *change management*, *time management*, and *leadership transformation* would complement the models you are implementing.

Reflecting

Time for reflection is essential because it allows us to step back and put our daily lives into perspective. For many principals, reflection takes place on the drive home from work. It is the best time to review the events of the day and what you learned. But it is also a time to transition to a more important focus—your family. Here's a trick I always used to practice reflection on the drive back home. Pick a halfway mark on your route and use it as the transition point. Between the times you get into your car and arrive at the halfway mark, reflect on the workday and then bring it to closure when you see the marker. Then use the rest of your time thinking about the family and how you can make them the center of your attention by the time you pull up the driveway. Principals ask a lot from their families and paying attention to reflecting on them will keep you centered and attentive to their needs. Make it a daily habit to transition yourself away from work before walking through the door. By the way, I reversed the process on the way to work by first thinking about my to-do list for the family, and at the halfway mark, reflecting on what I wanted to accomplish for the day on campus.

Training Alongside Teachers

There is a plethora of training opportunities for principals and your professional association offers quality programs that will enhance your leadership skills. But I have also found it useful to attend those conferences that are designed for teachers. First, they helped me sharpen my classroom skills so that I could stay out in front of new developments in curriculum, assessment, and instruction. Second, they offered me the opportunity to "go underground" and hear the perspectives and problems of teachers. This kept me grounded and sensitive to the challenges of teachers. Third, a side benefit was finding quality candidates for my next teaching opening in the school. I always collected cards, phone numbers, and addresses of teachers who impressed me at conferences and workshops.

Principals can also enhance their skills by taking advantage of some of the best executive training programs in the private sector. Most of the large cities host a variety of leadership seminars that offer quality training in topics that are applicable to school leadership. Many of these can be located by searching city convention and business service websites.

Finally, consider going back to school. In spite of the long hours and busy schedule, getting your next degree is doable, and for many, a career builder worth pursuing. Schools of education are constantly seeking ways of providing cohort programs that enable principals to pursue doctoral work on a calendar that fits with the work schedule. The journey is long and hard, but taking it alongside other educators is a worthwhile endeavor that will pay off throughout the remainder of your career.

Tracker Goals for Your Consideration: Expanding Knowledge and Skills

Shared Learning and Practice with Other Principals:

I will ...

1. Create my own professional learning community with other principals.
2. Develop a network of retired principals who can assist me in my school.

Action Research:

I will ...

1. Collaborate with teachers in the creation of an action research project that improves teaching and learning.
2. Partner with a local university to conduct a study of my leadership transformation.

Readings:

I will ...

1. Commit to increasing my reading of current news and developments in the field of education.
2. Scan multiple sources and select readings that connect with my needs.

Reflection:

I will ...

1. Practice reflecting on my daily work and relationship with my family.
2. Use my time on the way to work to mentally prepare for the day.

Training:

I will ...

1. Engage in professional training that improves my ability to lead and enhances my understanding of new developments in curriculum, instruction, and assessment.
2. Access the resources of my state association.

Chapter 15

Keeping Your Transformation on Track

The first and the best victory is to conquer self.

—PLATO

The central issue to any change in behavior is whether or not you can sustain it. In the first half of this book, we examined a process to inspect the daily habits and practices of principals and reduce the time invested in areas that contribute little to the improvement of teaching and learning in a school. In the second half, we investigated a model to help you spend more of your leadership in work that transforms yourself and engages others in providing children with higher levels of academic achievement and success. Change is difficult to keep on track, and in this chapter we will explore the overriding issues and themes that leaders must be attentive to in order to keep themselves and others on track. In a longitudinal study of principal interns, our research team discovered that aspiring principals feared that they would not be able to sustain instructional leadership once they move into formal leadership positions. Too often, they witnessed principals trying to change, but unable to sustain it (Berkey, Hutto & Berkey, 2008).

Sustaining Change in Your Leadership

By now you are probably asking yourself an important question:

"If I use these processes, how will I know if I am really changing my leadership?"

In working with a lot of principals, I have recognized a cycle of behaviors and feelings that interplay throughout their transformation. Figure 15.1 illustrates a series of stages that you will consciously and unconsciously move through as you implement the models presented in this book. You will know you are changing when you reach a level of awareness that you are pushing yourself through a continuous cycle that begins with a "launch" of a new practice, followed by an

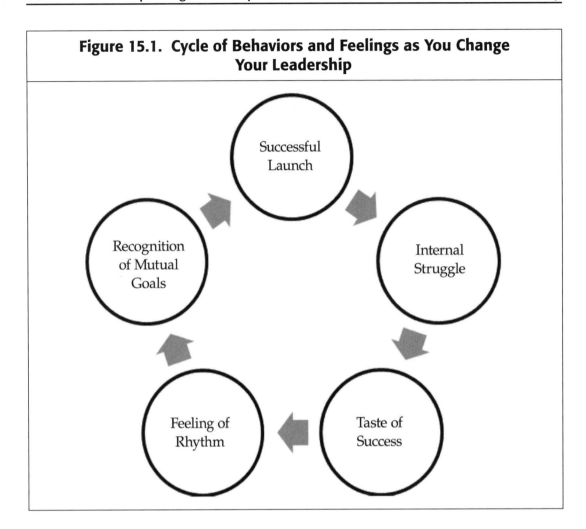

Figure 15.1. Cycle of Behaviors and Feelings as You Change Your Leadership

internal struggle to overcome resisters, a taste of success, a feeling that you have found a rhythm, and a realization that your leadership goals and those of the organization have become one. Let's review how this will happen in more detail.

Successful Launch

The overall strategy presented in this book is to decrease daily time in less effective areas of the principalship, while increasing time in those that bring substantive change and improvement to the school. To accomplish this shift, you should think of it as tipping the scales in increments as opposed to making big changes all at once. Using the leadership audit/analysis/transformation model, select an existing practice that you want to diminish and set up a SMART goal that will bring you quick results. An easy place to begin is with general office practices that keep you occupied while school is in session. Working with your secretary, establish a plan to free up an hour per day. This may appear to be a considerable amount of change, but most principals have been successful in accomplishing this in their first week of transformation. Why? It's like the person who loses the initial pounds in a diet. These are the easiest to shed, but important ones because they produce quick results that keep you focused.

At the same time you free up an hour of office work, remember the other half of the equation. This is the critical part of a successful launch because we all know how quickly the time can be consumed by other events and distractions. In your preparation work with the Tracker, start with Observing and Coaching the Learning Process by making classroom walk-throughs your first priority. Remember that part of the initial work is to engage the faculty in a collaborative discussion and design of the process so that when you appear in classrooms, teachers will understand that you are beginning your own transformation.

Internal Struggle

As you free up an hour each day and use it to visit classrooms, you will begin to go through an internal struggle that is a natural part of changing behavior. Much like the aches and pains of beginning an exercise regimen, a variety of thoughts and feelings will come into play. Many of them will represent barriers to sustaining your plan:

Fear: What will happen if my secretary doesn't know what to do?
        Will this change damage my leadership?
        What if teachers reject my increased presence in classrooms?
Guilt: Have I unloaded my responsibilities on others?
        Will people feel they have fewer opportunities to access my office?
        Are teachers going to think I have all the answers for their classrooms?
Pain: I still have to clean up office work when I return.
        Teachers are spreading rumors about my visits to their classrooms.
        I feel the culture pushing back on my transformation.
Doubt: Can I really do this?
        Will I really be able to commit to an hour per day?
        Will teachers really embrace walk-throughs in the long run?

Overcoming these struggles will make or break your transformation, and the single and most important response to these feelings must be addressed with what I consider to be the most essential ingredient of leadership.

Courage must always be the response when we struggle with decisions and actions in leadership. It is driven by two other components that cause people to be effective leaders: passion and vision. Our passion for transforming the role of the principal is ultimately energized by feelings that we have for our students. We know that schools must do a much better job of preparing children if they are to succeed in a world that is rapidly changing. Combining those feelings with a clear vision of what needs to change builds courage to act.

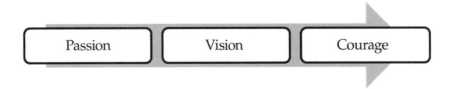

As you struggle with a variety of the aches and pains of change, remind yourself that you are doing it for children and that you have the confidence in the path to get you there.

Taste of Success

Nothing spurs people on like a taste of success. As the days go by you will begin to observe that things are working. Your secretary has stepped up to the plate and takes pride in demonstrating that things around the office went on without you. You have to spend less time at the end of the day with missteps that occurred while you were out in the building. Teachers have started to respond in a positive way to your walk-throughs and others have asked when you are coming to their classrooms.

You will begin to feel confident about visiting classrooms and providing feedback about each teacher's efforts to meet the vision of the school. And perhaps the most powerful force in this part of the cycle is the comfort level that you experience in being where the real work of the school takes place. Classroom walk-throughs become your favorite part of the work day.

Don't forget to invest in reflection. This is the time to use the first half of the drive home to think about the success you are having and the impact of your leadership. There is no doubt that you will start to feel more driven by purpose in your work.

Feeling of Rhythm

At some point you will recognize that the daily practice you have introduced is becoming a habit. That's a great sign that you are driving the plan to a deeper level and believing that you can sustain it over time. During this part of the cycle, principals begin to tinker with the effectiveness of their strategies and find ways to improve them. For example, in reducing the time spent on general office work, the principal and secretary get into a rhythm that becomes so efficient that it causes them to look for additional work that can be compressed. They target the volume of incoming e-mails and decide that the secretary can eliminate many of the "junk mail" messages by providing her access and authority to delete them while the principal is conducting walk-throughs.

The rhythm also extends to the areas that are the targeted for increased time. In this example, let's say you are getting very efficient in visiting classrooms and providing short notes to teachers. You would like to add a brief face-to-face encounter as a follow-up and begin to think about how you select classrooms in your daily walk-throughs. Up to now, you just picked them at random or looked for open doors. You realize that if you select teachers who have conference time toward the end of your hour of walk-throughs, you might be able to visit with them. This causes you to continuously change the time of day that you conduct walk-throughs so that you can have access to all teachers for a post- walk-through conversation.

Finding your rhythm has many benefits, and as we have discussed, it provides opportunities to practice at a level that transforms your practice from efficient to effective. It also leads into the last part of the cycle where you connect your change with that of the culture.

Recognition of Mutual Goals

As principals begin to tip the scales in their daily practices it provides an opportunity to address the purpose of their transformation:

How will my transformation bring change to the school?

In this part of the cycle, principals begin to realize connections to the vision of the school and opportunities to engage people in collaborative goals that move the culture in the right direction. For example, let's go back to the sample vision we have used throughout this half of the book and think about what happens when a principal uses classroom walk-throughs on a daily basis. As the principal provides feedback notes and engages teachers in follow-up discussions that center on curriculum, assessment, and instruction, a mutual recognition of the need for changes will begin to evolve. The principal begins to become a firsthand witness to a plethora of issues that are common to most classrooms. Individual teachers begin to think about the triangle and the areas that fall short in their daily lessons. Energy begins to build, and the culture becomes ripe for change.

The principal begins to meet with grade level and department teams to discuss the vision and how they can set SMART goals to address mutual concerns. Teachers point out the short-term need to improve curriculum as well as a long-term need to embed more time into the workday to facilitate shared learning and practice. The principal recognizes that their goals are mutual:

♦ Improving the curriculum delivered in every classroom.
♦ Providing more time to work on the vision of the school.

The completion of the cycle leads right into the next go-around. The next cycle begins with the principal freeing up more time within the day to collaborate with teachers on improvements to the curriculum (short term) and the design of a new daily schedule to implement next year (long term) so that teachers have embedded time in the workday for collaborative work.

Sustaining Change in the School

As you transform your leadership and spend more time working to improve teaching and learning, your challenge will not be limited to leading changes, but equally important, sustaining them. Too often school leaders introduce initiatives without understanding how to shift the culture, manage change, distribute leadership, and embed continuous learning among the staff. All of these actions are critical to the long-term success of the school and have been mentioned throughout the previous chapters. Let's do a quick review so that we finish this journey with a clear sense of the challenges of ensuring that your leadership makes a difference in the long run.

Shifting the Culture

Early in the book we examined the benefits of using a 360° assessment to capture a picture of how the school perceives your leadership. The changes that leaders model in their own behavior can have a significant influence in getting the culture of the school to move in the same direction. Be sure to conduct a follow-up 360° as one of several means of determining if people are recognizing your growth. If you are making gains, it follows that you are also moving the culture.

Bring attention to progress. Be aware of any work that aligns with the vision and quickly bring it to the attention of the school. This will remind people of what you value and expect to see. Spend time in your communications and meetings with teachers to praise collaborative work in the improvement of curriculum, assessment, and instruction.

Don't start battles. It will be tempting to take on resisters and saboteurs, but trust that eventually the culture will take care of these issues as people see the benefits of working together. Effective leaders move beyond the rhetoric and look for pockets of support that emerge within the culture. Spend time nurturing those who embrace the vision and avoid the negative people.

Demonstrate patience. Treat the culture like you would expect to be treated. Things won't happen overnight and impatience will only contribute to stress and anxiety among those who are attempting to change. Some weeks will feel like you are making progress, while others will feel like the school is in a mode of resistance. Wait for results.

Encourage experimentation and risk taking. Teachers have been weighed down with policies, procedures, and expectations that give them the impression that they can't be trusted to make any changes in their classrooms. Central offices have put undue pressure on teachers to comply with mandates that are supposed to enhance results on state assessments. This is a tough issue, and principals will have to make an extraordinary effort to ensure teachers that they will not be punished for making mistakes when trying new approaches and strategies.

Look for short victories. Nothing produces confidence like a win. Finding gains in the short term provides a validation to the culture that the vision is worth pursuing. But be careful with this. Make sure that the victory being claimed is for real. Teachers cringe when school leaders declare victory when it really didn't happen. This is why the principal should look for claims that originate with teachers and validate them before celebrating them.

Strengthen Relationships. Perhaps the best ingredient for sustaining a shift in the culture is the establishment of strong and meaningful relationships. The principal must set the standard by building personal relationships that are rooted in an unwavering commitment to children. Avoid transactional relationships that give the staff the impression that all you want from them is compliance. Effective principals invest considerable time in monitoring and massaging the relationships between members of the staff. Keep in mind that many teachers have worked in isolation, and as you bring them together, interpersonal skills will need to be developed.

Managing Change

Leaders in the field of change management have warned us that once you begin the change process, you can't control it (Kotter, 1996; Fullan, 2001). Instead, you must work with it and facilitate the process as best you can. One of the telling signs of leaders who understand this is their willingness to give up the permanent structures and processes that get in the way of the culture once the change process gets rolling. Some of the "sacred cows" that principals must let go of include the following:

Master Schedule: Several of the leading experts on the establishment of professional learning communities have emphasized the importance of designing daily schedules that enable teams of teachers to work collaboratively during time embedded in the workday (DuFour & Eaker). For most schools, this translates into a reorganization of the master schedule not only in terms of time, but arrangement of teaching schedules so that teams have common time together. Ask most principals or assistant principals about changing the master schedule and they dig in their heels. But without a willingness to change this structure, it will be nearly impossible to expect teachers to join hands on the path of school improvement.

Assignment of Staff: As teachers collaborate and recognize the need to provide flexible learning time for students, it will become obvious to many that there are more effective ways to utilize the skills and talents of staff, especially those in support roles. Principals must be willing to look at redistribution of special education staff, guidance counselors, teacher aides, curriculum specialists, and others who can help to deliver a more effective approach to helping each child reach mastery.

Budget: While principals have limited control of the portion of a campus budget that is flexible, giving teachers the opportunity to identify more effective ways to spend funds makes a lot of sense. Teachers can effectively identify needs that are more directly connected to the vision of the school and will look to the principal to facilitate this opportunity.

Staff Development: Schools send teachers to a number of workshops and training opportunities that don't always connect with the vision. This leaves other faculty members wondering if the principal was playing favorites or paying back a favor. As the culture of the school gets focused and begins to change, the issue of staff development budgets and staff development days will be raised. Principals must be willing to give control to teachers by setting the parameter that all staff development must be determined collaboratively and connected to the school's vision.

Distributing Leadership

Sustaining change requires shared leadership. The best proof of this is to examine schools that were able to remain on the path to school improvement after a principal moves on to another job. Effective principals transform their schools for the long run by distributing leadership throughout the culture. Every person in the school should be viewed as a potential leader. I can't count the number of times I have heard teachers state that they are more effective in the classroom because of the leadership training and experiences that were provided to them.

Bringing out the leadership in each person is not a difficult task and throughout this book you have been provided with numerous examples of how to give people the authority and responsibility to influence the vision of the school. Let's examine a few of the opportunities to distribute leadership that will emerge as you change your own leadership:

Need for Change: Some people will be so energized by these issues that they will step forward and volunteer to help facilitate additional presentations and communication.

School Vision: Teachers will step forward to lead discussions that pinpoint the specifics of the vision and offer their expertise in helping colleagues improve curriculum, assessment, and instruction.

Delegation of Principal Duties: Support staff will take pride as they see themselves in charge of areas that they previously saw themselves as just players.

Teacher Leadership: Teachers will see the need for leadership within their teams and devise ways to share it.

The list can go on but you get the point. Opportunities to distribute leadership will be abundant. Your challenge will be to make certain that people get access to the training that will be needed to lead their colleagues. Many schools have teacher leadership programs and if you don't, the investment is worthwhile. There are a wide variety of programs available, including private sector companies, universities, educational service centers, and state professional organizations.

The Sustained Journey

My purpose in writing this book was to stand at a crossroads in the evolution of the school principalship and point toward a better path, not because I have all of the answers but because I was one of the lucky ones. I had the fortunate opportunity of being pulled off the old path and mentored by some great principals who dared to blaze their own trails and guide me in a different direction. Many colleagues remained on the old path and became frustrated when the results went flat. They blamed it on the kids, the parents, and the faculty. They preferred to talk about their athletic teams rather than academics. Some retired only to be hired back by districts that don't see the future and how much things must change in order to prepare our children.

Our profession has been deluged with a sea of initiatives and ideas that are overwhelming to the professionals who have to serve in the front lines. The workshop circuits are full of people who promise that they have the right answer or the magic program. The real truth is that there are none that can independently solve the challenges that are ahead. It will take strong leadership with a passion for change, a clear vision of what needs to happen, and the courage to stand up to a plethora of critics and saboteurs to do what is right. To those with the courage, I offer my respect and hold high hopes for their leadership. Effective principals make a difference.

References

Archer, J. (2004). Tackling an impossible job. *Education Week*. Retrieved February 12, 2008, from http://www.edweek.org/ew/contributors/jeff.archer.html.

Barth, R. (1990). *Improving schools from within*. San Francisco: Jossey-Bass.

Bellamy, G. T., Fulmer, C. L., Murphy, M. J., & Muth, R. (2007). *Principal accomplishments: How school leaders succeed*. New York: Teachers College Press.

Berkey, T. (2008a). *The expectation gap: Conflicting roles of school principals*. Manuscript submitted for publication.

Berkey, T. (2008b). Strategies for transforming the daily work of principals: A study of present habits and opportunities for change. In R. Papa, C. M. Achilles & B. Alford (Eds.), *Leadership on the frontlines: Changes in preparation and practice* (pp. 266 (273). Lancaster: Proactive Publications.

Berkey, T. (2008c). Seize the day: Taking charge of how you spend your time can lead to improved student learning. *Principal Leadership*. 8(6): 22–26.

Berkey, T. & Dow, E. (2008). Texas school beats the odds with a shared commitment to student learning. *Journal of Staff Development*. 29(4): 31–34.

Berkey, T. & Hutto, N. (2008). Preparing teachers to lead sharing and practice. *PDS Partners*. 4 (1): 4, 9.

Berkey, T., Hutto, N. & Berkey, B. (2008). *Transforming the Principal Internship*. Manuscript submitted for publication.

Bridgeland, J.M., Dilulio, J.J. Jr., & Morison, K.B. (2006). *The silent epidemic*. Civic Enterprises in association with Peter D. Hart Research Associates for the Bill & Melinda Gates Foundation. Retrieved September 2, 2008 from http://www.gatesfoundation.org/nr/downloads/ed/thesilentepidemic3-06final.pdf.

Brown, J.H. & Brown, D. (2005). Why "at risk" is at risk. *American School Board Journal*. 192(11): 44–46.

Buckingham, M. & Coffman, C. (1999). *First, break all the rules*. New York: Simon & Schuster.

Cleveland Plain Dealer. (2007, October 24). Wal-Mart opens at steelyard commons with prayers and early birds.

Collins, J. (2001). *Good to great*. New York: Harper and Row.

Covey, S.R. (1989). *The 7 habits of highly effective people*. New York: Simon and Schuster.

Cumming, G.R., Goulding, D., & Baggley, G. (1969). Failure of school education to improve cardio-respiratory fitness. *Canadian Medical Association Journal*. 101(2): 69–73.

Davis, S., Darling-Hammond, L., LaPointe, M., & Meyerson, D. (2005). *School leadership study: Developing successful principals*. Stanford, CA: Stanford University, Stanford Educational Leadership Institute.

Danielson, C. & McGreal, T.L. (2000). *Teacher evaluation to enhance professional practice*. Alexandria, VA: Association for Supervision and Curriculum Development.

DePree, M. (1989). *Leadership is an art*. New York: Dell Publishing.

DuFour, R. & Berkey, T. (1995). The principal as staff developer. *Journal of Staff Development*. 16(4): 2–6.

DuFour, R. & Eaker, R. (1998). *Professional learning communities at work*. Bloomington, IN: Solution Tree.

Ferrance, E. (2000). *Action research*. Providence: Northeast and Islands Regional Educational Laboratory at Brown University.

Fiore, N. (1989). *Overcoming procrastination*. New York: MJF Books.

Friedman, T.L. (2007). *The world is flat: A brief history of the twenty-first century*. New York: Farrar, Straus and Giroux.

Fullan, M. (2001). *Leading in a culture of change*. San Francisco: Jossey-Bass.

Fullan, M. (2008). School leadership's unfinished agenda. *Education Week*, 27(32): 36, 28.

General Accounting Office. (2003) *Youth illicit drug use prevention: DARE long-term evaluations and federal efforts to identify effective programs*, United States General Accounting Office, January 16, 2003 (No. GAO-03-172R) : Author.

Gottesman, B. (2000). *Peer coaching for educators*. Lanham, MD: The Scarecrow Press.

Hess, F. M., & Kelly, A. P. (2005) *The accidental principal*. Stanford: CA: Stanford University, Hoover Institution.

Kise, J.A.G. (2006). *Differentiated coaching*. Thousand Oaks, CA: Corwin Press.

Knaus, W.J. (1998). *Break the procrastination habit . . . now*. New York: Barnes & Noble.

Kotter, J.P. (1996). *Leading change*. Boston: Harvard Business School Press.

Kouzes, J.M. & Posner, B.Z. (1995). *The leadership challenge*. San Francisco: Jossey-Bass.

Kouzes, J.M. & Posner, B.Z. (2003). Encouraging the heart: A leader's guide to rewarding and recognizing others. San Francisco: Jossey-Bass.

Lencioni, P. (2002). *The five dysfunctions of a team*. San Francisco: Jossey-Bass.

Leithwood, K., Seashore-Louis, K., Anderson, S., & Wahlstrom, K., (2004). *How leadership influences student learning: Learning from the leadership project*. The Wallace Foundation.

Levine, A. (2005, March). *Educating school leaders*. Washington, DC: The Education Schools Project. Retrieved October 5, 2007, from http://www.edschools. org/ reportsleaders.htm.

Lowe, E. (2008). *How to delegate effectively*. Edward Lowe Foundation. Retrieved 6-15-08 from http://www.edwardlowe.org/index.elf?page=sserc&storyid=6401&function= story.

Maxwell, J.C. (1995). *Developing the leaders around you*. Nashville: Thomas Nelson Inc., Publishers.

National Association of Secondary Schools (2001). *21st century school administrator skills assessment*. Reston, VA.

National Association of Secondary Schools. *NASSP Leadership Skills Assessment*. Retrieved 9-2-08 from http://www.principals.org/s_nassp/sec_inside.asp?CID=39&DID=39.

National Association of Secondary School Principals & Milken Family Foundation (2001). *Priorities and barriers in high school leadership: A summary of findings*. Retrieved January 8, 2008, from http://www.principals.org.

National Study of School Evaluation (2005). *Technical guide to school and district factors impacting student learning*. Schaumburg, IL.

Nonaka, I. (1994). A dynamic theory of organizational knowledge creation. *Organizational Science*, 5(1): 14–37.

Nonaka, I. & Takeuchi, H. (1995). *The knowledge-creating company*. New York: Oxford University Press.

Oakes, Jeannie. *Keeping Track: How Schools Structure Inequality*. Yale University Press, 1985. Woolfolk, Anita. 8th ed. Educational Psychology.Boston: Allyn and Bacon, 2001.

O'Dell, C. & Grayson, C.J. (1998). *If we only knew what we know*. New York: The Free Press.

O'Neill, K., Fry, B., Hill, D., & Bottoms, G. (2003). *Good principals are the key to successful schools: Six strategies to prepare more good principals*. Atlanta, GA: SREB. Retrieved January 31, 2008 from http://www.sreb.org/programs/hstw/publications/pubs/GoodPrincipalsKey.asp.

Patterson, K., Grenny, J., Maxfield, D., McMillan, R., & Switzler, A. (2008). *Influencer: The power to change anything*. New York: McGraw-Hill.

Peters, T.& Waterman, R. (1982). *In search of excellence: Lessons from America's best-run companies*. New York: Harper and Row.

Sanders, W. & Rivers, J. (1997). Cumulative and residual effects of teachers on future student achievement. University of Tennessee Value-Added Research and Assessment Center, Knoxville, Tennessee.

Santelli, J., Ott, M., Lyon, M., Rogers, J., Summers, D., & Schleifer, R. (2006). Abstinence and abstinence-only education: A review of U.S. policies and programs. *Journal of Adolescent Health*, 38(1), 72–81.

Sarafino, E. P. (2001). *Behavior Modification (2nd ed.)* Boston: McGraw-Hill.

Schlechty, P.C. (2001). *Shaking up the school house*. San Francisco: Jossey-Bass.

Schmoker, M. (1994). Tipping point: From feckless reform to substantive instructional improvement. *Phi Delta Kappan*, 85(6), 424–432.

Senge, P. (1990). *The fifth discipline*. New York: Doubleday.

Smith, H.W. (1994). *The 10 natural laws of successful time and life management*. New York: Warner Business Books.

Vollmer, J. (1994). *Why our schools need to change*. (Available from Local Control Project).

Warren, R. (2008). *The purpose driven life*. Lake Forest, CA: Saddleback Resources.

Wallace Foundation (2006, September). *Leadership for learning: Making the connection among state, district and school practices*. New York. Retrieved January 3, 2008, from http://www.wallacefoundation.org.

Waters, J.T., Marzano, R.J., & McNulty, B.A. (2003). *Balanced leadership: What 30 years of research tells us about the effect of leadership on student achievement*. Aurora, CO: Mid-continent Research for Education and Learning.

Waters, T., & Grubb, S. (2004). *The leadership we need: Using research to strengthen the use of standards for administrator preparation and licensure programs*. Denver, CO: Mid-continent Research for Education and Learning.

Wein, H. (2000). Stress and disease: New perspectives. *Word on Health*. Retrieved September 2, 2008, from http://www.nih.gov/news/WordonHealth/oct2000/story01.htm.

Wiggins, G. & McTighe, J. (1998). *Understanding by design*. Alexandria, VA: Association for Supervision and Curriculum Development.

Zepeda, S. (2003). *The principal as instructional leader*. Larchmont, NY: Eye on Education.

Appendix A

Principal's Job Description/Effective Principal Tracker

SCHOOL PRINCIPAL

Job Description

Primary Function: The primary function of the Principal is to ensure the adequate academic growth of each student through collaborative processes with staff and ongoing improvements in the delivery of curriculum, assessment, and instruction.

Responsibilities:

A. Setting and Shaping Expectations
1. Presents a clear and compelling case for the need to change public education to staff and members of the school community on an ongoing basis.
2. Focuses the culture of the campus on a shared purpose of high expectations for teaching and learning.
3. Engages teachers in a vision of the school shaped around an agreement on the expected standards for every classroom in the delivery of curriculum, assessments, and instruction.
4. Engages staff, administration, students, and parents in the vision of the campus and the support required by teachers to ensure the success of every student.
5. Strengthens relationships among all members of the school community in order to advance the vision of the campus.
6. Serves as an advocate and protector of the time and resources necessary for teacher collaboration and student learning.
7. Recruits and selects highly qualified teachers who embrace the vision.

B. Creating Disequilibrium
   1. Promotes growth and improvement by asking key questions and raising expectations at appropriate times.
   2. Models change by working on a daily basis with teachers to improve teaching and learning.
   3. Minimizes daily time on managerial tasks in order to maximize time in classrooms and collaborative work with teachers, teacher leaders, and teams of teachers.
   4. Distributes authority and responsibility of managerial tasks to others on campus.
   5. Prioritizes daily work with a focus on teaching and learning and protects time during student contact hours for engagement with teachers and learners in the classroom setting.
   6. Manages change by working with staff and school community to plan, implement, evaluate, and modify improvements to teaching and learning.

C. Engaging Staff in Knowledge Transfer
   1. Leads teachers in the design, selection, and implementation of processes and systems that enable professionals to share critical knowledge of effective curriculum, assessment, and instructional processes in a timely manner.
   2. Provides teacher teams with embedded time in the workday to design lessons and transfer best practices in instruction to each other.
   3. Involves teachers in the early identification, recruitment, and selection of high quality teacher candidates.
   4. Works with teachers and staff to analyze and transfer timely data to key professionals for adjustments to student learning processes.
   5. Engages teachers in collaborative processes to refine curriculum and transfer best practices throughout the staff.
   6. Collaborates with teachers to develop systems and processes to ensure valid and reliable assessment of and for student learning on a regular basis.

D. Observing and Coaching the Learning Process
   1. Performs frequent classroom walk-throughs to assess the quality of curriculum, instruction, and assessment processes employed in classrooms.
   2. Provides ongoing feedback and coaching to teachers to improve instructional delivery.
   3. Encourages teachers to experiment with new approaches to optimize the learning of each student.
   4. Listens to the concerns of teachers and collaborates on resolving learning problems of students.
   5. Serves as an advocate for reaching all learners and differentiating approaches to the content and processes in the classroom.

6. Mentors new teachers and helps them become equal partners on teacher teams.

7. Maintains high expectations for all parties to the learning process.

8. Collaborates with teachers, teacher leaders, and teams of teacher to set and attain specific goals that improve teaching and learning.

E. Expanding Knowledge and Skills

1. Seeks and transfers knowledge of best practices with other school principals and leaders.

2. Uses action research to experiment with new ideas, innovations, and processes that improve leadership capacity.

3. Engages in professional reading to expand knowledge and skills of best practices in school leadership.

4. Collects feedback from supervisors, colleagues, staff, and members of the school community to reflect on leadership effectiveness.

5. Models the ability to evaluate one's self and make improvements to performance.

6. Actively listens to teachers and staff to expand instructional leadership skills.

Secondary Function: Many of the responsibilities of the principal are not personally delivered but require oversight. The tasks and duties associated with these responsibilities are delegated and/or shared with staff throughout the campus.

Responsibilities:

1. Ensures the maintenance of a safe and orderly environment for learning.

2. Oversees the implementation of school and district policies and practices.

3. Coordinates the delivery of services to students, staff, parents, and community.

4. Provides delivery and supervision of campus events.

5. Manages the budget and purchasing processes.

6. Promotes good communication among all members of the school community.

Appendix B

Principal's Job Description/Educational Leadership Policy Standards:

ISLLC 2008 (National Policy Board for Educational Administration)

SCHOOL PRINCIPAL

Job Description*

Primary Function: The primary function of the Principal is to provide instructional leadership that improves student achievement.

Responsibilities:

A. **Vision of Learning (Standard 1)**
   1. Works with stakeholders to establish and practice a common vision and mission.
   2. Gathers data to drive goals, evaluate school performance, and share knowledge.
   3. Establishes and enacts plans to accomplish goals.
   4. Encourages ongoing and lasting growth.
   5. Assesses gains and makes adjustments.

---

*Based on the Educational Leadership Policy Standards: ISLLC 2008 as adopted by the National Policy Board on Educational Administration (NPBEA).

B. Advocate of School Culture and Instructional Program (Standard 2)
1. Promotes shared decision making, healthy relationships, and high expectations.
2. Establishes a quality curriculum that is comprehensive and rigorous.
3. Promotes a school culture that successfully engages students in learning processes that address their unique needs.
4. Supervises teaching.
5. Creates assessment processes and data systems of student learning.
6. Enhances the instructional leadership skills of staff.
7. Provides greater time for effective instruction.
8. Advocates for the integration of technology that enhances teaching and learning.
9. Assesses the effectiveness of the instructional program.

C. Management of Operations and Resources (Standard 3)
1. Oversees and assesses the operations of the campus.
2. Accesses, deploys, and assigns all personnel, financial, and technology resources.
3. Maintains a safe and orderly school campus.
4. Grows and distributes leadership among staff.
5. Provides and protects time for effective teacher collaboration and student learning.

D. Collaboration with Staff and Community (Standard 4)
1. Gathers and evaluates feedback relative to the school environment.
2. Recognizes and accesses the various resources of the community.
3. Develops and maintains healthy relationships with members of the school family.
4. Develops and maintains healthy relationships with members of the school community.

E. Leadership with Integrity, Fairness, and Ethics (Standard 5)
1. Establishes a means making the system responsible for the academic and social success of each student.
2. Models self-improvement and ethical practices.
3. Ensures democratic values and equal opportunities for all.
4. Uses legal and moral lenses to evaluate the outcomes of decisions.
5. Advances the issues of fairness and centers the work of the school on the needs of students.

F. Management of the Culture (Standard 6)
1. Serves as a mentor for students and families.
2. Engages in local, state, and national issues that impact education.
3. Maintain awareness of internal and external forces and navigate changes to advance the vision of the school.

Appendix C

References for the Effective Principal Tracker

Listed below are some of the references that were taken into consideration in the development of the Effective Principal Tracker. Many of these sources overlap in terms of conceptualization and implementation. While not an exhaustive list, it includes several of the leading contributors in the respective fields.

Setting and Shaping Expectations

The Moral Imperative of School Leadership, Michael Fullan
The Leadership Challenge, James M. Kouzes & Barry Z. Posner
Leading Change, John P. Kotter
Leading in a Culture of Change, Michael Fullan
The 7 Habits of Highly Effective People, Stephen R. Covey
Influencer, The Power to Change Anything, Kerry Patterson, Joseph Grenny,
    David Maxfield, Ron McMillan, & Al Switzler
Shaking Up the School House, Phillip C. Schlechty
Building Leadership Capacity in Schools, Linda Lambert
The Five Dysfunctions of a Team, Patrick Lencioni
The Principal Challenge, Marc S. Tucker & Judy B. Codding (Editors)

Creating Disequilibrium

Good to Great, Jim Collins
First, Break All the Rules, Marcus Buckingham & Curt Coffman
The Leader of the Future, The Drucker Foundation
Inventing Better Schools, Phillip C. Schlechty
Change Leadership, Tony Wagner, Robert Kegan, Lisa Lahey, Richard W.
    Lemons, Jude Garnier, Deborah Helsing, Annie Howell & Harriette
    Thurber Rasmussen
Results, the Key to Continuous Improvement, Mike Schmocker

Paradigm Lost, Reclaiming America's Educational Future, William G. Spady
Who Moved My Cheese?, Spencer Johnson

Engaging Staff in Knowledge Transfer

If We Only Knew What We Know, Carla O'Dell & Jack Grayson, Jr.
The Faster Learning Organization, Bob Guns
Professional Learning Communities at Work, Richard Dufour & Robert Eaker
Reculturing Schools as Professional Learning Communities, Jane Bumpers Huffman & Kristine Kiefer Hipp
The Adaptive School: A Sourcebook for Developing Collaborative Groups, Robert J. Garmston & Bruce M. Wellman
Deciding What to Teach and Test, Fenwick English
A New Vision for Staff Development, Dennis Sparks & Stephanie Hirsh
Creating Great Schools, Phillip C. Schlechty
The Principal as Instructional Leader, Sally Zepeda
Understanding by Design, Grant Wiggins & Jay McTighe

Observing and Coaching the Learning Process

Enhancing Student Achievement, A Framework for School Improvement, Charlotte Danielson
Preparing Teachers for a Changing World, Linda Darling-Hammond & John Bransford (Editors)\
Evaluating Professional Development, Thomas R. Guskey
Leading for Learning, Carl D. Glickman
Peer Coaching for Educators, Barbara Gottesman
The Learning Leader, How to Focus School Improvement for Better Results, Douglas B. Reeves
The Three-Minute Classroom Walk-through, Carolyn Downey, Betty E. Steffy, Fenwick English, Larry E. Frase & William K. Poston, Jr.
The Art & Science of Teaching, Robert J. Marzano
Teacher Evaluation to Enhance Professional Practice, Charlotte Danielson & Thomas L. McGreal
The Power of SMART Goals, Jan O'Neill & Anne Conzemius
Instructional Leadership, 2nd Edition, Anita Woolfolk Hoy & Wayne Kolter Hoy
Teaching in America, Gerald Grant & Christine E. Murray
Teachers as Leaders, Perspectives on The Professional Development of Teachers, Donovan R. Walling, Editor
The High Performing Teacher, Avoiding Burnout and Increasing Your Motivation, Lee Canter & Marlene Canter

Expanding Knowledge and Skills

360° Feedback, The Powerful New Model for Employee Assessment & Performance Improvement, Mark R. Edwards & Ann J. Ewen

The 10 Natural Laws of Successful Time and Life Management, Hyrum W. Smith

Getting Things Done, The Art of Stress-Free Productivity, David Allen

Overcoming Procrastination, Neil Fiore

Leading with Soul, Lee G. Bolman & Terrence E. Deal

The Principalship, A Reflective Practice Perspective, Thomas J. Sergiovanni

Becoming a Reflective Educator, How to Build a Culture of Inquiry in the Schools, John W. Brubacher, Charles W. Case & Timothy G. Reagan

Reflective Practice to Improve Schools, An Action Guide for Educators, Jennifer York-Barr, William A. Sommers, Gail S. Ghere, & Jo Montie

Studies That Influenced the Tracker

Preparing School Leaders for a Changing World: Lessons from Exemplary Leadership Development Programs, Stanford University, Final Report, Linda-Darling Hammond, Michelle LaPointe, Debra Meyerson, Margaret Terry Orr, & Carol Cohen

Preparing School Principals: A National Perspective on Policy and Program Innovation, Institute for Educational Leadership & Illinois Education Research Council, Elizabeth L. Hale & Hunter N. Moorman

Balanced Leadership: What 30 Years of Research Tells Us About the Effect of Leadership on Student Achievement, Mid-continent Research for Education and Learning (McREL), Tim Waters, Robert J. Marzano & Brian McNulty

Schools Can't Wait: Accelerating the Redesign of University Principal Preparation Programs, Southern Regional Education Board, Betty Fry, Kathy O'Neil & Gene Bottoms

The Principal Internship: How Can We Get It Right? Southern Regional Education Board

Assessing Learning-Centered Leadership, Vanderbilt University, Ellen Goldring, Andrew C. Porter, Joseph Murphy, Stephen N. Elliot & Xiu Cravens

The Autonomy Gap, Barriers to Effective School Leadership, American Institute for Research & Thomas B. Fordham Institute, Steven Adamowski, Susan Bowles Therrialut & Anthony P. Cavanna

Appendix D

PLC Team Assessment

Indicators of an Effective Professional Learning Community

Team Assessment

☐ Demonstrates a shared vision defined by what is expected in each classroom.

1	2	3	4	5
Never	Almost Never	Sometimes	Almost Always	Always

Comments: _____

_____

☐ Achieves repeated short-term gains over extended periods of time and reports these to colleague, leadership, students, and parents.

1	2	3	4	5
Never	Almost Never	Sometimes	Almost Always	Always

Comments: _____

_____

☐ Uses trial and error to improve curriculum, assessment, and instruction.

1	2	3	4	5
Never	Almost Never	Sometimes	Almost Always	Always

Comments: _____

_____

☐ Engages members in ongoing diagnosis and treatment of student learning problems.

1	2	3	4	5
Never	Almost Never	Sometimes	Almost Always	Always

Comments: _____

_____

☐ Expects all members to identify, transmit, evaluate, access, and implement best practices.

1	2	3	4	5
Never	Almost Never	Sometimes	Almost Always	Always

Comments: _____

_____

☐ Establishes daily time for members to come together to plan, restructure, refine, and improve curriculum, instruction, and assessment.

1	2	3	4	5
Never	Almost Never	Sometimes	Almost Always	Always

Comments: _____

_____

☐ Promotes incremental improvements in teaching and learning through a sense of urgency and value added for each student.

1	2	3	4	5
Never	Almost Never	Sometimes	Almost Always	Always

Comments: _____

_____

☐ Collaborates with other teams and individuals to strengthen articulation of learning experiences for each student.

1	2	3	4	5
Never	Almost Never	Sometimes	Almost Always	Always

Comments: _____

_____

☐ Builds relationships with other teams and exchanges best practices with them.

1	2	3	4	5
Never	Almost Never	Sometimes	Almost Always	Always

Comments: _____

_____

☐ Engages members in self-reflection and relationship building to strengthen the work of the team.

1	2	3	4	5
Never	Almost Never	Sometimes	Almost Always	Always

Comments: _____

_____

☐ Builds strong relationships between the home and school.

1	2	3	4	5
Never	Almost Never	Sometimes	Almost Always	Always

Comments: _____

_____

☐ Expects results that are confirmed by internal and external audits.

1	2	3	4	5
Never	Almost Never	Sometimes	Almost Always	Always

Comments: _____

_____

☐ Identifies team dysfunctions and works to improve relationships.

1	2	3	4	5
Never	Almost Never	Sometimes	Almost Always	Always

Comments: _____

_____

☐ Measures team performance and hold itself accountable.

1	2	3	4	5
Never	Almost Never	Sometimes	Almost Always	Always

Comments: _____

_____

Appendix E

PLC Tools

Learning by Doing, A Handbook for Professional Learning Communities at Work
  Richard DuFour
  Rebecca DuFour
  Robert Eaker
  Thomas Many
    2006 Solution Tree
    Bloomington, IN   ISBN 1-932127-93-3

Reculturing Schools as Professional Learning Communities
  Jane Bumpers Huffman
  Kristine Kiefer Hipp
    2003 Scarecrow Education
    Lanham, Maryland   ISBN 1-57886-053-9

Multimedia Communities of Practice Training Toolkit
  American Productivity and Quality Center
    123 North Post Oak
    Third Floor
    Houston, TX 77024

Leading Professional Learning Communities: Voices from Research & Practice
  Shirley M. Hord
  William A. Sommers
    2007 Corwin Press
    Thousand Oaks, CA   ISBN 9781412944779